Two con
Change your life

LifeSigns®

How are You? Really.

Scott C. Watson
Introduction by Dan Davis

Fourth Edition, Revised and Expanded Hopevale Version
© 2020 LifeSigns Partners, Inc.
Learn more at myLifeSigns.org

LifeSigns: Two Conversations that Will Change Your Life
Copyright © 2020 by Scott C. Watson
LifeSigns® is a registered trademark of Relevant Labs, LLC, all rights reserved.

Published by LifeSigns Partners, Inc., Frisco, Texas, United States

For information about LifeSigns® assessments, books, consulting, and research, please visit myLifeSigns.org.

Library of Congress Cataloging-in-Publication Data
Watson, Scott, 1966 –
    LifeSigns: how are you? really : two conversations that will change your life / Scott Watson. Fourth edition. Hopevale version.
    p. cm.
    Included bibliographical references.
    ISBN: 978-1-7343700-1-0 (softcover)
    1. Spiritual life—Christianity. 2. Christian living. 3. Spiritual assessment. I. Title.

All scripture quotations, unless otherwise indicated, are taken from the *Holy Bible: New International Version*®. NIV®. Copyright © 1973, 1978, 1984 by International Bible Society. Used by permission. All rights reserved.

All rights reserved. No part of this publication may be reproduced, stored in a retrieval system, or transmitted in any form or by any means—electronic, mechanical, photocopy, recording, or any other—except for brief quotations, without the prior permission of the publisher.

Printed in the United States of America

 Use the camera in your smartphone to read the QR codes throughout this book (see sample left). Try it! For example, this QR code block will take you to Hopevale.org/LifeSigns.

DEDICATIONS:

To Pete Briscoe, who taught me about
Life with Jesus.

To Paul Miller, who taught me about
Life with People.

To Matt McGinnis, who taught me about
Life with Purpose.

What's it like to take your LifeSigns?

"I have never talked to God in this way and it was easier for me to identify what I needed to say to him."

"I really liked the sense of talking to God one-on-one. I really felt like He was sitting right beside me! Pretty intense! That this might be a chance to really move forward with my spiritual growth and walk. I'm feeling pretty hopeful!"

"Thank you for making me think about these tough issues. I only cried twice!"

"It was like I was having a conversation with my beloved Savior. As if I could feel His arms around me as I was laying my heart out on the table before him."

"I loved feeling like I was talking to God. I liked the way the questions were worded. I felt like I was having a conversation with my Lord."

"It made me dig deep into what I really feel. I know I couldn't lie because I was talking to God and He knows how I feel."

"Wow, I thought it was great! It made me realize I can be totally honest with God, I opened up to him more. I know He already knows my situation, but it helps to write it down. I feel better already."

"LifeSigns was awesome for me because I was actually able to pinpoint WHY for myself when I felt conflicted on something. I felt like I could be more honest."

Contents

Foreword by Paul Miller iii
Acknowledgements v
Introduction by Dan Davis vii

Part I: The Why, What, and How of LifeSigns

Why take your LifeSigns? 1
The Two Conversations 11
A Candid Conversation Guide 21

Part II: Twelve Candid Conversations

Conversation One: Life with People 33
Conversation Two: Life with Jesus 49
Conversation Three: Life with Purpose 63
Conversation Four: Work Life 87
Conversation Five: Looking for Work 101
Conversation Six: Student Life 115
Conversation Seven: Money and Finances 127
Conversation Eight: Healing and Grace 147
Conversation Nine: Married Life 161
Conversation Ten: Parenting 181
Conversation Eleven: Hurtful Habits 197
Conversation Twelve: Single Life 219
The Last Chapter: Take a Step of Faith 229

Appendices

Appendix A: Frequently Asked Questions 247
Appendix B: Methodology of LifeSigns 251

Foreword: by Paul Miller

This book is an invitation.

Years ago, I received a similar invitation. Early in my ministry career, the invitation came from a leader who became a mentor, who became a friend, who became a brother. It was through that friendship that I learned the importance of honest conversation, and authenticity with God and with others.

I was part of a team of ten guys serving together in a vibrant student ministry at a church in Chicago. Our leadership team would get together every Thursday morning at 6:00 AM, and the conversations were honest and authentic (and a bit caffeinated). We were not allowed to skim across the surface of how we were doing. Our leader challenged us to go deeper. He modeled authentic leadership for us. Along the way, I got my first real taste of community—and the power of authenticity. Ever since those formative years I have tried to create environments that would invite those I serve with and lead to experience the same thing.

LifeSigns is an invitation to honest conversation.

Foreword

When I first met Scott Watson, he was a key leader in a new ministry I was stepping into, and we quickly became friends. We had the privilege of working together in the early stages of a process that ultimately led to the creation of LifeSigns. Our goal was simply to encourage candid conversations, vertically and horizontally. We knew that if people took the time to have an honest conversation with God, followed by honest conversations with trusted friends, they would begin to experience the Life that Jesus had for them—the abundant Life He promises in John 10:10.

I hope you'll lean into the LifeSigns process. It's really just an invitation into two honest conversations: first with God and then with a trusted friend. And I hope you allow this book to help guide you in those conversations. It can help you and your friends, or your small group, or you and your spouse to experience Life.

I hope you accept the invitation. Trust me, it's worth it.

Paul Miller
Executive Pastor, Hopevale Church

Acknowledgements

I'm not the first person to fall in love—with a church. Just listen: Is this not the passionate prose of a man in love?

> *"I always thank my God for you...I long to see you...it is right for me to feel this way about all of you, since I have you in my heart...God can testify how I long for all of you with the affection of Christ Jesus...you whom I love and long for, my joy and crown...open wide your hearts."*

When you read this mash-up of bits and pieces of letters written by the apostle Paul to churches in Rome, Galatia, Philippi, Colossae, Thessalonica—even to that unruly bunch of believers down in Corinth—it's clear Paul is head-over-heels in love.

Twenty-some years ago, fresh out of grad school and new to the metropolis of Dallas-Fort Worth, an old college roommate invited me to visit Bent Tree Bible Fellowship. I arrived at this oddly named church, housed in an odd-looking building, squeezed among the suburban sprawl of houses and strip centers along Midway Road. The parking lot was full, the halls were crowded, and the narrow staircases were overrun with rambunctious kids.

After that first Sunday, I knew this church was "the one."

A lot has changed over the last two decades: twenty-fold growth, three new campuses, and a vibrant on-line community. But one thing remains the same: The heart of Bent Tree still beats

ACKNOWLEDGEMENTS

steady and strong for Christ, and Christ alone. That's why I love my church. Even today, she's beautiful to me. Through all the changes and growth pains, I've had a front-row seat as she's blossomed from awkward adolescence into flowering maturity.

You may think it's strange to speak of Jesus' church in such affectionate, if not romantic terms. But remember, in addition to being His children, the church is also His bride, purchased with His blood, awaiting a spectacular marriage with Jesus in heaven.

So, my gratitude for my home church of Bent Tree is placed first and foremost at the feet of Christ. My pastor and longtime friend, Pete Briscoe, led her faithfully for 28 years with a strong hand and a soft heart. Many, many of the insights woven throughout this book can be traced right back to decades spent under Pete's masterful teaching. Pete taught me what it means to be alive in Christ, and how Christ is alive in me.

Thank you, Pete. I love you.

And thank you to my crack team of editors, including Michelle Attar, David Dobat, Carol Laird, Paul Miller, Susan Shumake, Kevin Stilley, Richard and Cindy Watson, Julie Weeks, and Eric Willis. A sincere thank you to those who read the entire manuscript, including Pete, Michelle, Mom, and Dad. You've all spared readers from my reckless grammar, while offering fresh and discerning feedback. A special thank you to pastor Michelle Attar for holding me up in prayer when tears blurred the screen and covered the keyboard. To this day, Michelle gently reminds me that, in God's skillful hands, my brokenness is also a major reason for my usefulness.

Finally, I need to acknowledge someone posthumously: the apostle Paul. His passion for Christ and zeal for the church bursts from the pages of his letters in vivid detail. When I meet him one day in glory, I'm going to tell him, "Thank you, Paul, for writing it all down."

LifeSigns has given me the chance to love the church and express the Life of Christ in ways I'd never imagined. I'm just grateful that Jesus has finally helped me to write it down.

Introduction

How We Grow at Hopevale

Before jumping into your "horizontal conversations" with LifeSigns, I'd like to take a minute to answer a fundamental question: How do we grow at Hopevale?

Jesus said, "I have come that they may have life, and have it to the full." (John 10:10)

Jesus' words aren't just a fanciful wish; they are a hopeful promise that speak to the deepest places of longing in our hearts. Jesus came, died, and rose again so that we could enter into His capital "L" LIFE and experience that LIFE to the absolute fullest. This LIFE begins by placing our faith in Jesus—to know Him not as just *a* Savior but *our* Savior.

This choice involves giving up trying to be perfect in order to please God and choosing instead to trust fully in Jesus and His perfection. His perfection covers our imperfection. It only happens by God's grace through our faith in Jesus Christ. That is how we *become a Christian*. This life-changing choice is available to each one of us, and it's an essential first step if we want to experience all that God has for us.

Introduction

But as amazing as it is for us to take that first step into full life, that's just the beginning. There is so much more of His LIFE for us to experience, both in this life and the life to come. The Hopevale LIFE Model helps to explain what it means to *grow as a Christian* and become more like Jesus (see below).

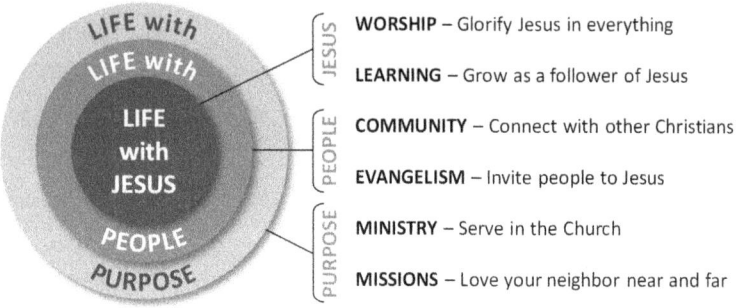

LIFE with Jesus, LIFE with People, LIFE with Purpose

Let's start at the core. Once we know Jesus personally as our Savior and desire to follow Him more fully as our Lord, LIFE with Jesus becomes THE primary relationship for us. It's a relationship marked by these two priorities: First, LIFE with Jesus means we Glorify Jesus in Everything with a comprehensive faith, not a compartmentalized one. So, LIFE with Jesus isn't just confined to one hour on a Sunday; rather, it's reflected in our desire to honor Jesus every hour of our week—all 168 of them—and in every area of our lives. This is our gift of gratitude to Him. Second, LIFE with Jesus also means we Grow as a Jesus-Follower, where we passionately pursue learning more and obeying better as His disciple, with the goal of becoming more and more like Him in our everyday lives. That is LIFE with Jesus.

From that foundation comes our LIFE with People. It is not good for any of us to be alone. We're all created in the image of

God and built for relationships because God Himself (Father, Son, and Holy Spirit) is relationships. So, a natural outflow of our LIFE with Jesus is our LIFE with People, both within the church and beyond the church. Within the church, we need to <u>Connect with Other Christians</u>, which means forging genuine, relational connections with others in the church, so that the LIFE with Jesus within us can flow back and forth between us in mutually encouraging ways. Then beyond the church, God sends us out to <u>Invite People to Jesus</u> so they can experience the capital "L" LIFE that He has for everyone. We do this by sharing good news, by spreading good deeds, and by living good lives. What an opportunity each of us has to represent Jesus in our daily lives, wherever God has placed us. Living this life in relationship to others inside and outside the walls of Hopevale is part of the abundant life Jesus has promised us.

This then leads us to our LIFE with Purpose and the call to live for something so much bigger than ourselves. We do that in a couple of different ways. First, we <u>Serve in the Church</u> following the example of Jesus Himself who came not to be served, but to serve. God gives every Christian a special place in the body of Christ and unique gifts to serve others as channels of His life-giving grace. When we all show up in the specific ways He's gifted us, the Body of Christ works best and reflects His glory. It's amazing to be a part of that here at Hopevale! Second, we also <u>Love Our Neighbor Near and Far</u> and play our part in helping to fulfill Jesus' Great Commission to make disciples of all nations— in our local community, in the Great Lakes Bay Region, and around the world.

This is God's growth plan for all of us, but how do we make it practical? Well, you can't get to where you want to go unless you first know where you're starting. That's where LifeSigns comes in. LifeSigns is an invitation to two honest conversations that will change your life—a vertical conversation with our personal, loving

Introduction

God followed by a horizontal conversation with a trusted friend. Those conversations are built upon one little question with big implications: "How are you? Really?"

So, I'm excited to take this LifeSigns journey with you. I truly believe Jesus will honor our honesty with God and trusted friends to lead us into greater experiences of His LIFE like never before. I can't wait to see what God will do!

Dan Davis
Senior Pastor, Hopevale Church

Part I:

The Why, What, and How of LifeSigns

Chapter One

Why Take Your LifeSigns?

*"The Lord does not look at the things people look at.
People look at the outward appearance,
but the Lord looks at the heart."*
- God speaking to Samuel

S CENARIO #1: If you see me at church on a typical Sunday morning, the conversation usually goes something like this:

"Hey Scott, how are you?" you ask.

"I'm fine. How are you doing?" I'll say.

You'll reply, "I'm great. Busy! Lots going on. So, how's work and the kids?"

I'll smile, "Oh, business is finally looking up. And the kids are growing up so fast!"

"Well, it's really good to see you," you reply.

"You too. Take care!" And off we go.

Chapter One: Why take your LifeSigns?

Here's Scenario #2:

Now let's say you're someone I truly trust, like my friend Paul Miller, who knows me and loves me anyway—which is a bigger deal than you'd imagine. We're sitting at breakfast, making small talk. The food has just arrived.

Paul leans forward and says, "Okay bro, we haven't talked in ages. You've been avoiding me, haven't you? I want to know, how are you?" After a moment of silence, he adds, "Really."

"I know, I know. I've been busy," I say. "You really want to know?" (long pause...) "To be honest, it's been the most difficult year of my life."

Paul looks me in the eye and says, "Listen buddy, I care about you. What's going on? Just shoot straight with me—no pat answers allowed."

Cautiously, I test the waters. "Well, the economy forced us to lay off most of the employees, and my business partner left, so I've assumed his share of the corporate debt. I'm putting in some long hours at work. Then I blew-out my ankle, so I have not been running, and I've gained about 20 pounds. Okay, it's closer to 25 pounds."

Paul's eggs are getting cold and he doesn't even notice. He's totally locked-in and listening. I take a deep breath and open the door a little wider.

"Okay, here's where I'm at today. You may have heard that after 20 years of struggle and counseling, my marriage is over. So now I've got the kids much of the work week. I haven't figured out how to juggle client projects, cleaning the house, laundry, homework, and business travel. Most of the time, I just feel totally on my own: I'm alone at work, alone on brutal deadlines, alone raising the kids, alone with all the debt, and . . . I'm alone every night in that big empty bed. Life is really hard right now."

Paul says, "I'm sorry buddy. That explains a lot. So, what I really want to know is this, how's it going with you and Jesus?"

Does he see my handshake as I take a sip of coffee? "I wish you wouldn't ask me that question..."

I swallow hard and tell him, "I know that Jesus will never leave me or forsake me, and the Bible says He's an 'ever-present help in time of need,' but to be honest Paul, on most days I can't seem to find Him. I'm sure He's there. We just don't talk like we used to. I'm in survival mode right now."

I press on: "Sometimes at night, instead of reaching for my Bible or the phone to call you, I grab a beer or two (or three) from the fridge and hit the couch. The gap between what I believe and how I behave is painfully wide, and it's getting wider. I know all this stuff about Jesus is true, but as I continue to struggle, I get the feeling there must be something deeply wrong with me. Sometimes, I think God must be angry with me. My life feels broken, and I can't seem to fix it. That's how I'm doing. Really."

In both scenarios, you've asked me the same question, *but gotten two radically different answers.* What's the deal?

It's not that deep conversations don't happen at church—they happen all the time. But right before the service, when everyone's in a hurry, it's difficult to go deep. Especially if you're hurting.

The Purpose of LifeSigns

The purpose of LifeSigns is to help you figure out how much you're *experiencing the amazing, abundant life of Christ.* That's it. The challenge is that we all get busy, distracted, or wounded—so we become isolated from God and from those around us. LifeSigns is designed to help you honestly connect with Christ and to be honest with people who love you.

We know that, "the Lord doesn't look at the things people look at. People look at the outward appearance, but the Lord looks at the heart" (1 Samuel 16:7). God sees beneath the surface. He's intimately acquainted with all your ways. He knows your thoughts from afar. Before there's even a word on your lips, He knows it all (see Psalm 139).

Faking it doesn't work with God. So why do we fake it with each other?

Chapter One: Why take your LifeSigns?

LifeSigns is two candid conversations that will change your life: first with God, and then with someone you trust. LifeSigns conversations can feel risky because they fly in the face of our culture, one that values "the outward appearance" of polish and success—especially on social media.

LifeSigns is about authenticity, up close and personal. It's about dropping your guard and being honest is a way that is Biblical and safe.

A Visit with the Great Physician

In many ways, taking your LifeSigns is like taking your vital signs at the doctor's office—we're making an intentional analogy. Your four physical vital signs—temperature, blood pressure, pulse rate, and respiratory rate—are outward indicators of your inner health. Those four objective, physical measures can tell a doctor a lot about what's going on *inside your body*.

In a similar way, the Bible contains hundreds of the "signs of life" in Christ. LifeSigns puts key scriptures into the familiar context of your everyday world, and encourages you to ask God to, "Search me and know my heart, try me and know my anxious thoughts; and see if there's any hurtful way in me, and lead me in the everlasting way" (Psalm 139).

In fact, we used Psalm 139 as the framework for LifeSigns: asking God to search your heart, test your mind, and lead you forward. LifeSigns gives you a set of reliable, Biblically based indicators of your spiritual health. Since your spiritual health is as important as your physical health, at least once a year it's a good idea to meet with the Great Physician and ask Him to examine your spiritual health. When you do, you'll learn a lot about what's going on *inside your heart.*

And just as your doctor can spot a problem and prescribe steps to greater health, so too with LifeSigns. *It's both descriptive and prescriptive.* You're getting both a snapshot of your current spiritual health, as well as specific Biblical recommendations, so you can take the next steps in your walk with Christ.

LIFESIGNS: HOW ARE YOU? REALLY.

Not taken LifeSigns yet?
Visit Hopevale.org/LifeSigns

Note: Use the camera in your smartphone to read the QR code (the box above). It will take you directly to the website or video.

WHERE DID LIFESIGNS COME FROM?

When my home church opened a shiny new 3,500-seat worship center attendance nearly doubled. Our elders and pastors were thrilled—and worried. They began asking some difficult questions: "Are we a mile wide and an inch deep? Are new people connected in community—or just consumers? Do they have any idea how to grow in Christ?" These concerns were justified, because more than 50% of our regular attenders were not connected to the church in a meaningful way.

So, in 2008, my church assembled a cross-functional team to tackle the problem, headed by pastor Michelle Attar. Michelle challenged us: "We need to help everyone evaluate their current spiritual health and identify next steps in their Christian walk. In order to reach everyone, we need a flexible, online spiritual assessment tool, supported by coaching, that can be repeated on a yearly basis."

So, our little project team collected surveys from a dozen prominent churches. We met and prayed. We collated and debated, amassing a library of 300 potential questions. But nothing stuck. None of it felt like "us." Out of frustration, we started over with a blank sheet of paper. The result was something radically different from a church survey—LifeSigns.

As far as we know, there's nothing quite like LifeSigns available today—and it's got Jesus' fingerprints all over it. Let me explain. You've heard that only God's grace can take something dead and make it alive. As with Joseph who faced calamity in Genesis, only God can take something evil and use it for good.

Chapter One: Why take your LifeSigns?

Only Jesus can take something broken and turn it into something whole and useful. Only Him.

So, where did LifeSigns come from? *A broken life made new.*

As you may have already guessed, everything in the two scenarios at the beginning of this chapter is true about me, Scott Watson. As I wrote this book, we had long discussions about whether I should share parts of my story with you, or just write a generic book with generic examples. Obviously, we've decided to include some carefully selected parts of my messy life.

Here's why: This book isn't about me. *It's about you, and it's about the redeeming work of Christ.* There are three good reasons it's appropriate and helpful to share real life stories, they're the same reasons we're encouraging you to share your story through your LifeSigns experience.

Reason #1: We All Need Authenticity

First, as they often say in recovery groups, "God never wastes a hurt." Unfortunately, I've got first-hand experience with a difficult marriage, divorce, single parenting, business and financial struggles, past abuse and addictions, poor choices, and even doubting God's goodness. Many of those awful experiences show up in the LifeSigns questions. Can you relate to one or two of those issues?

The struggles and failures in my life have driven home the critical need for honesty with God and with people I trust.

While it's embarrassing to share my stuff with you, we know that God's redeeming grace, "causes all things to work together for good to those who love Him, and who are called according to His purpose" (Romans 8:28). And once the initial version of LifeSigns was created, dozens of people at my home church allowed God to use their "issues" to make LifeSigns even more practical and relevant.

If God were not in the business of miraculously turning our trials into His treasure, LifeSigns as we know it wouldn't exist. We'd have just another boring church survey.

Have you ever felt broken or isolated because of your secret struggles? Then LifeSigns was created just for you.

Reason #2: We Need Christ's Power

Second, the Bible says that God's strength is revealed in our weakness. Weird, huh? Once the apostle Paul figured this out, he said, "So now I am glad to boast about my weaknesses, so that the power of Christ can work through me" (2 Corinthians 12:9).

Okay Paul, let me get this straight. We're to "gladly boast" of our weaknesses? I still wrestle with that one. But it's amazing how God seems to enjoy using the "foolish things and weak things, the lowly things of this world" for His glory (1 Corinthians 1:27-28).

Let me ask you: Is it possible that your greatest area of struggle, the thing you've been avoiding or hiding from the world, may actually be your greatest opportunity to fully experience God's grace? This has been true for me with LifeSigns.

Consider for a moment: *What if God wants to impact the world through you, not in spite of—but because of your struggles?*

Reason #3: We Need God's Grace

Third, God's grace is unleashed in humility. More than once the Bible says, "All of you, clothe yourselves with humility toward one another, for God is opposed to the proud, but gives grace to the humble" (1 Peter 5:5). With LifeSigns, we're just trying to practice what we preach. How could we offer you a book about authenticity without being authentic? How could we ask you to humble yourself without practicing a bit of humility ourselves?

Here's the point: LifeSigns conversations can be humbling, if you're willing to be honest.

No, you don't have to spill your guts to everyone you meet in the church lobby. *That's not appropriate.* But when you take the risk and humble yourself with God and someone you trust, there's a magnificent response directly from the throne of heaven. The Bible says that after a season of struggle and suffering, "the God of

Chapter One: Why take your LifeSigns?

all grace, who called you to His eternal glory in Christ, will *Himself* perfect, confirm, strengthen and establish you" (1 Peter 5:10).

That's a powerful promise. There is freedom in honesty.

Think about it: When the walls of pride are toppled, the God of all grace sits up and takes notice. When you choose to humble yourself, God personally leaps into action in your life. As you'll see, this spirit-enabled cycle of humility and grace is one of the recurring themes of LifeSigns.

LifeSigns is About Real Life

Real life is not as neat and tidy as our carefully curated social media profiles might suggest—so let's not pretend that it is. You don't have to put on a happy face and act like everything is just peachy if it's not. With LifeSigns, you can be yourself.

My pastor, Pete Briscoe, loved to remind us, "Life is too short to pretend. Besides, pretending is exhausting."

To contrast, honesty is freeing.

So, it really doesn't matter if you know about some of Scott's embarrassing junk. That's not who I am. My failures don't define me. My identity lies elsewhere, *and so does yours.* While I was born Scott Charles Watson in Cleveland, Ohio on July 11, 1966, the Bible says that I have been, "crucified with Christ and it's no longer I who live, but Christ who lives in me" (Galatians 2:20). God has made me a new person, holy and blameless in His sight, justified, sanctified, renewed, and redeemed by the blood of the Christ (2 Corinthians 5:17).

Hey, that's not spiritual double-speak, it's rock-solid truth. A radical transformation has taken place in my life—I'm just learning how to walk in it. So, I've made up my mind to stop pretending and hiding, because, as the apostle Paul discovered, Christ's power is unleashed in my weakness.

So, let me ask you: *Are you hiding?*

If you've bowed your knee to Christ as Lord, you're new too. It's safe to come out now. Your true identity is defined by Christ, not by your bad choices, wounds, or messy circumstances. God has exchanged your hurts for His holiness. That's how this Jesus thing works.

The phrase "abundant life" is more than a clever punch line used by preachers to woo the unconverted; it's the very essence of why Jesus made the trip to earth—and to the cross. He said, "I came that they may have life, and have it abundantly" (John 10:10). It's His mission—and it's your birthright as a believer.

Our LifeSigns team is praying that you'll place yourself in the loving and gentle hands of the Great Physician. God will lead you through this process to deep places, to broken places, to all the hidden stuff that's been buried in your busy life. He'll also point you toward a future and hope. He will open your eyes and direct your steps (Proverbs 16:9).

You can trust Him, even if you're not quite sure about trusting other people yet.

One more thing: *LifeSigns isn't just about analysis, it's about action.* You'll find that God will nudge you out of your comfort zone. Please just follow Him. Make up your mind right now: You'll do whatever He tells you to do. Make difficult phone calls, have awkward conversations, tell people you're not okay—even if it's scary and humbling. Dealing with important stuff always is.

As you uncover your true identify in Christ, I promise—better yet—God promises on the precious blood of His only Son, you will "experience Life" like never before.

Ready to experience Life? Then let's go.

Chapter Two

The Two Conversations

"The unexamined life is not worth living."
– Socrates, Athens, 401 B.C.

There was a rhythm to Jesus' life.

In the middle of busy public ministry, at odd hours, Jesus would steal away from the crowds for one-on-one time with the Father. His disciples were confused by His disappearances, and quite frankly, a little miffed. One time, "Simon and his companions went to look for Him, and when they found Him, they exclaimed: 'Everyone is looking for you!'" (Mark 1:36). That's the biblical equivalent of: "Where the heck have you been?" Upon His return, Jesus provided His disciples with fresh insights from the Father and new direction for ministry.

CHAPTER TWO – THE TWO CONVERSATIONS

I've noticed this same rhythm at work in the lives of mature Christians. From time to time, they sense the tug of the Spirit to "come away" and spend some unhurried time with the Father. Busy schedules, yard work, soccer games—nothing deters them. Extended time with the Father finds a protected place on the calendar, even when other people don't understand. When they return, they talk about what happened in their time with God, usually with a spouse or trusted friend. With fresh insights and new direction, they make changes and reap the benefits of walking in sync with the Spirit.

It may be common sense, but it's not common practice.

THE PROBLEM: FRAGMENTATION AND ISOLATION

Fragmentation and isolation are two fancy words that mean we all get: 1) busy and 2) disconnected.

First, how does our life become fragmented? Overloaded schedules and overloaded senses are two of the main culprits. Spiritual things are squeezed-out by a schedule already filled to the brim with work, parenting, travel and other priorities. Even in our down time, something is always screaming for our attention: social media, unanswered e-mail, unwashed dishes, or kids who need help with homework. No wonder it's so hard to focus!

Second, we become isolated when we're too busy to invest time to cultivate deeper relationships. It's ironic: With social media, we've never been more connected—and never felt more isolated. There are other reasons we find ourselves alone in a crowd. When you're hurting, there's a basic human tendency to withdraw. The more you hurt, the more you'll hide. The same is true when you're struggling to break free from a hurtful habit. Like Adam and Eve after the fall, we feel ashamed, so we hide from God and from people who love us. Have you ever felt wounded and isolated at the same time? It's an unhealthy combo.

LifeSigns is about relationships. It was deliberately designed to counteract both busyness and loneliness.

Step one, the "vertical conversation," helps you to connect with Christ in the middle of a busy, fragmented life. Step two, the "horizontal conversation," combats isolation by showing you how to open-up with other people. Through it all, God's grace makes it safe to stop hiding and start growing. So first, LifeSigns is a candid conversation with the God who made you, knows you, and loves you anyway. Then, as you're honest with God, you'll find it's much easier to be honest with another person. That's one way LifeSigns can prompt new growth in your life.

Step One: The Vertical Conversation

It can be intimidating to even think about having an honest conversation with the Almighty God. You may not know where to start. In Psalms, David gives us a helpful framework for having a vertical conversation. Look at the last two verses in the chapter: *"Search me, O God, and know my heart; test me and know my anxious thoughts. And see if there be any hurtful way in me and lead me in the everlasting way"* (Psalm 139:23-24).

Notice the four verbs in this scripture: God is the one doing the searching, testing, seeing, and leading—not you. LifeSigns is not about self-evaluation, it's a conversation with your Heavenly Father who knows you better than you know yourself.

Watch an invitation to the vertical conversation at: Hopevale.org/welcome-to-lifesigns

What does a vertical conversation sound like? To be sure, one-on-one conversations with God are different for everyone, but hearing about other peoples' experiences is helpful. Plus, these

Chapter Two – The Two Conversations

may spark some ideas for your next vertical conversation with God:

"I could feel His arms around me as I was laying my heart out on the table before him."

"How wonderful to sit and hear God ask you questions you've been asking yourself for years. I was able to be still and get lost in a conversation about all the things that make up my life. It felt as if God and I were 'walking in the garden in the cool of the day.' How fabulous is that!"

"It made me dig deep into what I really feel. I know I couldn't lie because I was talking to God and He knows me. It was like I was having a conversation with my beloved Savior."

"Wow, it made me realize I can be totally honest with God, I opened up to him more."

"It made me dig deep. I know I couldn't lie because I was talking to God and He knows how I feel."

"I love the idea that MY Savior wants to spend time with ME and wants to know MY thoughts about how I'm doing and how I feel about our relationship. It also helps to quickly pinpoint the different areas of my life I feel really good about, and those I can work on."

"I have never talked to God in this way. It was easier for me to identify what I needed to say to him."

Did you know that God is intensely interested in your life? Go read Psalm 139 from start to finish sometime. Notice how intimately God knows everything about you: your past, your present, and your future. Your vertical conversation is a golden opportunity to connect with God and talk about, "How am I?

LifeSigns: How are you? Really.

Really." This includes everything from marriage to money, from wounds to work life. With LifeSigns, nothing is out of bounds.

When Christ breathed his last on the cross, the veil that separated the people from God's presence in the temple was ripped wide open, from top to bottom (see Matthew 27:51). It was as if in that moment the Father declared, "There is absolutely nothing standing between you and Me, except an open door."[1] Can you see how God paved the way for a deeper, more intimate relationship with you?

On Solid Ground: Saving Grace

What if you're not 100% certain that you even have a relationship with God? Perhaps you're still exploring and have questions. Maybe you've never actually said "Yes" to a relationship with Jesus. Then this may be the most important part of the LifeSigns process for you.

Learn how to have a relationship with Jesus in eight minutes:
Hopevale.org/Gospel

Jesus said, "For God did not send his Son into the world to condemn the world, but to save the world through Him" (John 3:17). If you want to begin a relationship with Jesus, just talk to God and let Him know:

> ➢ I believe that You love me. I believe that Jesus really is God who stepped down from heaven in the form of a sinless man to pay the penalty for my sin on the cross.
> ➢ I understand that my rebellion and sin has separated me from You, Lord, now and forever.

---

[1] Pete Briscoe, General Editor, *Christianity: A Follower's Guide* (Broadman & Holman Publishers, Nashville, Tennessee, 2001).

Chapter Two – The Two Conversations

> - I accept Your free gift of forgiveness, salvation, and new life through Christ alone. I trust you with my life.
> - From this day forward, I'm going to put You in the driver's seat, and trust You to live *in* me and *through* me.

Jesus said, "I tell you the truth, whoever hears My word and believes in Him who sent me has eternal life and will not be condemned; he has crossed over from death to life" (John 5:24). When you trust Christ alone for your salvation, *that is 100% true about you.* You may not feel radically different, yet God promises that He has come into your heart, forgiven your mistakes, and has made you a new person.

So now, as you engage in your vertical conversation with the Heavenly Father, remember that He lives in you and will never leave you.

Be sure to tell a Christian friend about your decision to begin a relationship with Christ. They'll be thrilled at your good news and can share ways to grow in your relationship with Christ. Also, check out NeedHim.org to learn more.

Step Two: The Horizontal Conversation

The Bible offers a wealth of wisdom on how to have a horizontal conversation with someone you trust. For some practical ideas and principles, see Chapter Three, "A Candid Conversation Guide."

At the beginning of the book of Romans, Paul the apostle is making travel plans. Several attempts to visit the believers in Rome hadn't worked out, so he wrote, "I long to see you. When we get together, I want to encourage you in your faith, but I also want to be encouraged by yours" (Romans 1:12). Paul understood the joy and necessity of connecting with other believers to find encouragement.

That sounds lovely, doesn't it?

Here's the problem: According to the latest batch of LifeSigns data, many people don't see it that way.

The very last question on LifeSigns asks you to pick from four options for your horizontal conversation: 1) with someone you trust, 2) a pastor, 3) a coach, or (4) on your own. When we examined the responses across those four options, here's what we found:

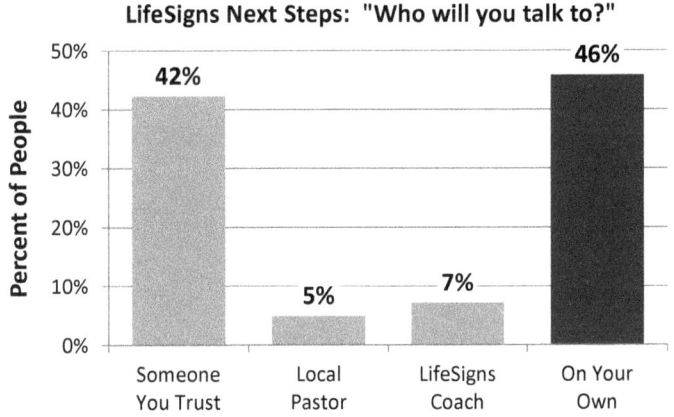

So what? If nearly half (46%) of people don't want to have a horizontal conversation, they can always explore their LifeSigns results on their own. I respect that decision. You don't have to share your LifeSigns results with anyone. Nobody is forcing you to do anything. It's also possible that 46% of people don't have someone they can trust. And if you don't belong to a church or attend a small group, it's hard to make a connection with someone spiritual and safe.

But you should know *there's a huge downside if you chose to "go it alone."*

We found a significant difference in the overall health of people willing to open-up to someone they trust, compared with those who said, "I'm on my own." People willing to talk about their LifeSigns results scored higher on 53 of 58 LifeSigns items. Said differently, in 91% of the areas covered by LifeSigns, people

CHAPTER TWO – THE TWO CONVERSATIONS

with someone to talk to are "doing better" than those who are alone (see graph).

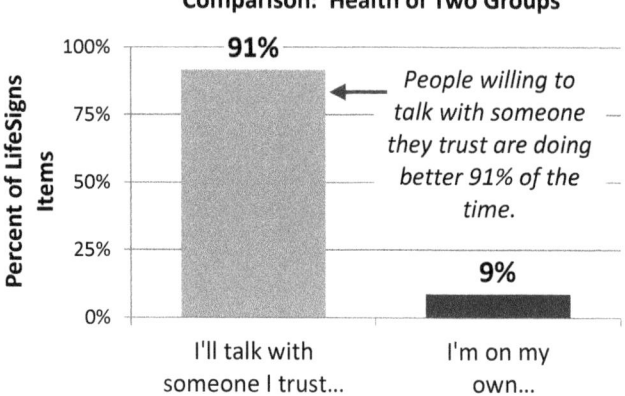

This is deeply concerning. Thousands of people who take LifeSigns are isolated, and by comparison, not doing as well as people who are connected. But there's more to this story, and it has driven me to tears and to my knees.

We did a statistical analysis to identify in which areas isolated people struggle the most. We discovered that the twenty biggest differences, when comparing people willing to share with "someone they trust" against people "going it alone," included *all eight* of the LifeSigns questions in the Marriage section. It also included *all six* items from the Healing and Grace section.

Those numbers are sobering. Here's why: The more you struggle in marriage, or the more you live with deep wounds, the more likely you are to become isolated and say, "I can handle this on my own." Isolation is one of the enemy's most effective weapons in his efforts to take you out.[2] We'll talk more about the vital importance of staying connected with people in the chapter on Relationships.

Here's the bottom line: Having a horizontal LifeSigns conversation takes courage—especially when the storms of life, or

---

[2] see 1 Peter 5:8-9, Ephesians 6

a rough patch in your marriage, have prompted you to batten down the hatches. Stop for a moment and consider: Who can be a safe harbor for you? Who can you talk to about the deeper issues in your life? Who could you call right now?

If no one comes to mind, you can always connect with a pastor or counselor at a local church. With most churches, just call the main number or visit the church website to ask for an appointment. Or, if you know someone who is also taking LifeSigns, see if they'll grab coffee and have their horizontal conversation with you. It could be the beginning of a great friendship.

When you take a risk and open-up, here's what happens:

"My horizontal conversation was freeing and life-giving. I was able to open up about some sensitive issues in my life."

"I was stuck. I didn't know what to do next. But our conversation helped me talk through the next step. I am so very thankful."

"My horizontal conversation was awesome. We are holding each other accountable to follow through on next steps."

"The conversation was healing, as I talked through the issues with my husband. Some of which we have discussed in the past, but with LifeSigns we went into greater detail."

"My horizontal conversation went well. As a result, I set some challenging goals to achieve my spiritual growth."

"LifeSigns helped me see the true need in my life to develop relationships where I can have honest conversations that can help me grow."

Chapter Two – The Two Conversations

Finally, you may be ready, willing, and able to have a conversation with someone you trust. That's great. Make this conversation a top priority in your busy schedule. And remember, the Bible says, "A friend loves at all times. He is there to help when trouble comes" (Proverbs 17:17).

Next Steps: Your Growth Priorities

If you've taken your LifeSigns, you should already have your 24-page Personal Growth Plan. Page four shows your self-selected priorities for growth, by topic. In the chapters that follow, the first few pages will get you thinking about the important issues in each section. Then you'll find discussion questions and scriptures for each LifeSigns item.

Where do you start? Anywhere you want!

You don't have to go in order, just flip to the chapter with the topic that interests you and dive into a candid conversation.

Chapter Three

A Candid Conversation Guide

"Because you listened to me, I knew that you really loved me."
- Jill Briscoe

Eighteen seconds.

Researchers at Johns Hopkins University studied thousands of recorded conversations between doctors and their patients. They found that, "on average, physicians interrupt patients within eighteen seconds of when they begin telling their story."[3]

---

[3] Jerome Groopman, M.D., *How Doctors Think* (Houghton Mifflin Company, New York, New York, 2007), p. 17.

Chapter Three – Candid Conversation Guide

It didn't matter if the doctor was a general practitioner, an internist, a surgeon, or a specialist—they all consistently and chronically interrupted their patients at the *beginning* of a consultation.

Why do most doctors, regardless of their specialty, interrupt patients so quickly? One of my physician friends assures me that interrupting is *not* part of the curricula in medical school, along with chemistry and anatomy. Yet doctors do tend to interrupt us, don't they?

I don't think it's because doctors are distracted. After all, they're focused on listening to only one patient at a time. Yes, they're often in a hurry, caring for dozens of patients in a single day—*but eighteen seconds?*

My theory about this annoying phenomenon is simple: doctors are diagnosticians. It's a physician's job to find and fix a problem. In their defense, making a thorough and accurate medical diagnosis demands rigorous inquiry. With your life and health on the line, they'd better ask lots of questions.

Here's the point: When it comes to a LifeSigns horizontal conversation, y*ou're not the doctor. Jesus is.* You're not supposed to "fix" anybody. Jesus does the fixing, and that can be tremendously freeing.

Candid Conversation Killers

LifeSigns conversations are a two-way street. The rest of this book is designed to help you candidly and safely talk about your inner life with somebody you trust. However, when the other person has the floor, you need to avoid three conversation killers at all costs: interrupting, judging, and offering unsolicited advice. Don't believe me? Try any of those with a spouse or friend, and then see what happens. The conversation will quickly grind to a screeching halt.

That's why a candid conversation—and especially a LifeSigns conversation—requires a different approach. When the other person is talking, your only job is to "Listen, Love, and Point."

You can't fix someone—only Jesus can. But you can listen to them, love them, and point them to Christ and to biblical truth.

Our little mantra to "Listen, Love, and Point" is easy to remember, but can be difficult to practice. So, let's spend a minute on each.

Making it Safe #1: Listen

I don't know if my pastor, Pete Briscoe, took advanced listening classes in seminary, but I can tell you this: Pete is one of the best listeners I've ever known. Even though he's incredibly busy, when we talk, I feel that he's 100% focused on our conversation. Can you guess Pete's listening secret? *It's because he loves me.* Two decades of friendship, through triumph and trials, have proven that Pete cares about me, not just my ministry. His attention flows from his affection.

That's why, in order to listen well, you must love well.

Good listening takes patience. Through dozens of candid conversations over the years, I've found that people tend to open-up slowly, revealing one layer at a time, holding back deeper matters of the heart until they know it's truly safe. The more painful or sensitive an issue, the more love and patience that's required. So, when your partner has the floor, if you jump in with some brilliant advice or share parts of your story, the door of dialogue will likely slam shut. The Bible reminds us that, "The purposes of a person's heart are deep waters, but one who has understanding draws them out." (Proverbs 20:5).

"No problem," you say, "I'm a great listener."

Are you sure? Can I shoot straight with you? *Bad listening is like bad breath.* Other people usually won't say anything about it; they'll just keep a safe distance.

I've got personal experience as a bad listener. One hot summer day on my 19th birthday, a college buddy wrote on the back of my birthday card: *"Scott, sometimes I cannot imagine Jesus talking the way you talk."* I was shocked. I was a little offended. But slowly, I began to realize he was right. As my mouth ran non-

Chapter Three – Candid Conversation Guide

stop, I ran right over people. All these years later, I'm grateful for my friend's candor about a blind spot. So, if you suspect listening is not your strong suit, a LifeSigns conversation provides a great opportunity to learn how to listen.

Here's something I've found helpful: If you're listening during a LifeSigns conversation, and you're just dying to interject a pearl of wisdom—*silently pray it, don't say it.* Turn your commentary heavenward, keep your ears open, and watch as God quiets your heart and returns your attention to the person sitting across from you.

Good listening also requires that you exercise discernment. A gentle and well-timed question can help someone dig a little deeper, opening the door a little wider. But you cannot force it open. Don't even try.

Good listening will cost you something. In my experience, listening with your whole heart requires intense, focused effort. With every sense and synapse, you strain to hear the cry of the heart, buried beneath the jumble of words. And when, by the power of the Spirit, you genuinely care about the person sitting across from you, listening can be effortless.

An excellent resource on how to have safe, productive conversations is called the "Speaker/Listener Technique," and is found in *A Lasting Promise: A Christian Guide to Fighting for Your Marriage* by Scott Stanley, et al.

Speaker/Listener Technique:
marriagemissions.com/speaker-listener-technique

Making it Safe #2: Love

Talking honestly about your life can be intimidating, even if you know someone pretty well beforehand. And as we've said before, when you're facing significant struggles, the urge to hide can be overwhelming. That's why candid conversations, ones that are safe and supportive, are built on a foundation of unconditional love and grace.

I can't say it any better than the apostle John: "There is no fear in love. But perfect love *drives out fear*, because fear has to do with punishment" (1 John 4:18-19). And that's the issue. You wonder if you'll regret opening-up. Will you be shamed, scolded, or judged? Or will you be embraced and encouraged?

Here's the good news: Nothing breaks the icy grip of fear and shame more quickly than a friend who looks you in the eye and says, "I just want you to know, I love you. I care deeply about you. And absolutely nothing you say today, nothing you share, can change that fact." That's how love "drives out fear."

In this context, notice how that famous passage about love in 1 Corinthians 13 also reads like a how-to manual for candid conversations: "Love is patient. Love is kind. It does not dishonor others, it is not self-seeking, it is not easily angered, it keeps no record of wrongs. Love does not delight in evil but rejoices with the truth. It always protects, always trusts, always hopes, always perseveres. Love never fails."

When you express Christ's love in a LifeSigns conversation, you *will* be patient with the other person. You *will* be kind. You'll protect people's privacy and honor them with your undivided attention. You'll hang in there, even when they start to ramble. Through it all, the person sitting across from you will experience God's love—and be transformed in the process.

You're just along for the ride. How cool is that?

MAKING IT SAFE #3: POINT

Listening and loving are essential elements in a safe candid conversation. When someone feels fully heard—and when they give you permission—you can also point them in the right direction. God can speak directly through you, because "the tongue of the wise brings healing" (Proverbs 12:18).

Chapter Three – Candid Conversation Guide

First, you can *point people to the truth*. Each of the 12 "Conversation Starters" in this book includes carefully selected scripture. The idea is to introduce God's voice into your LifeSigns conversation. You can simply say, "Thanks for sharing your heart with me. Let's see what the Bible says about that...", then turn to the scriptures together.

Second, you can *point people to Christ*. In Galatians we're told to "carry each other's burdens, and in this way, you will fulfill the law of Christ" (Galatians 6:2). That means you carry people with heavy burdens *to Christ*. Jesus is the great physician, the counselor, and the burden lifter—not you.

"Makes sense," you say, "but how does that work?"

True story: *Late one night, my cell phone jolted me awake. The caller ID showed it was Kevin, my good friend and accountability partner. My first thought? I sure hope nobody has died.*

"Hey buddy, what's up?" I mumble in a sleepy haze.

"Susan and I just had a huge fight," he said. "I lost my cool and said some really stupid stuff. And now she's throwing around the 'D-word' again. She wants a Divorce."

"I'll be right over," I said.

As I sat on the curb of my friend's house at midnight, he replayed the awful exchange, blow by blow, finally dissolving into sobs of despair. What a mess. I desperately wanted to help, but I knew there was nothing I could say in that moment to fix it. I threw a desperate prayer heavenward, "God, now what?"

Putting my arm around Kevin's slumped shoulders, through tears of my own, I said, "I love you buddy. I'm so sorry you guys are struggling. All I can do is point you to Jesus. He'll know what to do. Come on man, let's pray..."

It's like you're leading someone by the hand, guiding them up the steps to what the Bible calls, "the throne of Grace, so that we may receive mercy and find grace to help in time of need" (Hebrews 4:16). That's how you point people to Christ.

Finally, you can *point people to others who can help.* Obviously, if you think someone is a danger to themselves or others, or if a child is in danger, you've got to call for help. Day or night, you must make that call. You can dial 911, and then it's a good idea to call for backup (i.e., a friend, pastor, etc.). For other issues, you can always point people to a counselor, pastor, or doctor. Most of us need a little nudge to get moving in the right direction.

For most everything else, the individual LifeSigns pages in this book are filled with dozens of excellent, proven resources.

As we've said before, *LifeSigns is not just about analysis, it's about action.* As you wrap-up your horizontal conversation, identify your next steps, make specific commitments, and hold each other accountable in the days and weeks to come. You may even decide to put a candid conversation on your weekly schedule.

And be sure to check out the "Last Chapter" in this book to learn how to close the gap between your beliefs and your behaviors by taking a step of faith.

What About Marriage Issues?

A word of warning: Conversations about marriage are a minefield. It's never more important to "Listen, Love, and Point" than in a candid conversation about marriage issues. A few additional guidelines may be helpful, especially if you're a small group leader. Let's consider two scenarios.

Scenario #1: One-on-one conversations about marriage

In every marriage, remember there are two sides to every story. When a husband confides in you that, in spite of doing A, B, and C, she's still not responding, you may develop some strong opinions about his wife. Not so fast. Talk with the wife and you may discover that, the husband is not doing X, Y, and Z—all of which he failed to mention. This new information will throw the whole situation into a different light. Blind spots are prevalent in marital relationships. All couples have them. A trained counselor or pastor is often the best person to sort through a tangle of thorny marriage issues. So, when necessary, lovingly point the couple in that direction.

Scenario #2: Group conversations about marriage

If you're discussing the Marriage section of LifeSigns in a mixed small group, *we strongly recommend that you split up into separate groups of men and women.* Why? In our experience it's much easier and safer to discuss marriage issues in a same-sex group—without your spouse glaring at you from across the room. Trust me, I speak from personal experience on this one.

Once you're in same-sex groups, don't be surprised if you hear wild laughter coming from the ladies' side of the house. The guys will likely finish first and start talking about sports or power tools or whatever—all the while wondering what's so darn funny over there. For some reason, that's how this usually works.

Once you've had separate discussions as men and women, come back together and share your insights. If you're the group leader, lay down some ground rules and keep a firm hand on the conversation. Encourage people to share general insights, not highly personal issues with the full group. When you take this approach, people will feel safe and you'll have a rich discussion.

One more thing: If you see puffy eyes and Kleenex, be ready to follow-up with a side conversation.

WHAT'S IN THE REST OF THIS BOOK?

Each of the "conversation chapters" is designed to get you thinking and talking about important aspects of your life. These chapters are not intended to be a comprehensive discussion of all the issues related to, for example, marriage or getting out of debt. Instead we're using a combination of scriptures, LifeSigns insights, and personal stories to spark candid conversations about your personal situation.

LifeSigns: How are you? Really.

    LifeSigns is about *your story* and *your journey* with Christ. That's why you'll also find discussion questions, scriptures, and resources for each individual LifeSign at the end of each chapter. We want to stimulate an authentic, life-changing conversation between you and someone you trust. Sound good?

    Now, with a humble heart, armed with biblical truth, and in the ever-present love and grace of your heavenly Father, go for it. Share what's really going on. Drop the mask. Take a risk and become "known" to someone you trust. Don't forget to Listen, Love, and Point. Then watch as God does something wonderful in your life.

Part II:

Twelve Conversations that will Change your Life

Conversation One

Life with People

"Bubba was my best good friend."
- Forrest Gump

Remember the vivid scene from the movie?

Forrest Gump and his platoon are ambushed in the dense jungles of Vietnam. As hot lead rips through the air inches above their heads, deadly mortar rounds fall directly on their position. Clearly outgunned and overwhelmed by enemy fire, his friend Bubba yells, "Run Forrest, Run!" So, Forrest grabs his rifle and runs for his life, jumping over limbs and weaving through the dense undergrowth, dodging death with every step.

"I ran and ran," Forrest said, "I ran so far and so fast, that pretty soon I was all by myself, which is a very bad thing."

Yes Forrest, being alone in the jungle is *a very bad thing*.

CONVERSATION ONE – LIFE WITH PEOPLE

My pastor, Pete Briscoe, often reminds me that, "No one should do life alone." That's especially true when you're under enemy fire and running for your life.

THE DANGERS OF ISOLATION

One of our enemy's favorite tactics is isolation. He wants to separate you from God and from people who can help you. When shame or guilt makes you want to pull away from people, you're as vulnerable as an injured calf separated from the herd. That's why Peter warns us, "Be alert and of sober mind. Your enemy the devil prowls around like a roaring lion looking for someone to devour" (1 Peter 5:8). The implication is clear: Don't leave the herd and you won't get devoured.

What causes isolation? Perhaps you're busy and don't make the time to develop deeper relationships. Or, if you're carrying deep hurts and wounds, it can feel awkward to be around "normal people." Maybe you've been wronged in the past, and the fear of rejection paralyzes you. Or perhaps you've felt, as Adam and Eve discovered after the fall, that sin has created an overwhelming urge to hide (see Genesis 3:8-9). Or maybe you're a strong and independent person, so you don't like to depend on other people. You can handle life on your own.

Do any of these reasons for isolation ring true for you?

Unfortunately, I can relate to just about all of them. A number of years ago, running a start-up company squeezed out most of my non-essential relationships. The pain and shame of a failing marriage made it difficult to be around happy couples. My intermittent struggles with addiction and depression were carefully managed, and yes, concealed. And my natural inclination to be strong and responsible made me reluctant to ask anyone for help.

Yet in the darkest moments, I yearned to "become known" to someone I could trust and who could help. (For more on dealing with hurts, see Conversation Eight: Healing and Grace.)

LifeSigns: How are you? Really.

The fact is, no matter how busy or independent you are, there's no such thing as the lone wolf Christian. You were created to be connected. Even God once said, "It is not good for man to be alone" (Genesis 2:18).

"But life with people can be messy," you say. "Relationships take time and effort. And even then, people don't respond positively, or worse, they take advantage of you."

All true. So why bother?

LifeSigns Insights: A Case for Community

If you've attended church for some time, it's easy to develop an indifference to "churchy things." For example, you may not think a small group could make much of a difference in your life. After all, participating in a church-related small group represents a relatively small slice of your weekly pie. You may assume that attending a group or Bible study is nice, but couldn't possibly impact the rest of your modern, jam-packed, highly caffeinated life.

And you'd be wrong.

The LifeSigns research on "Life with People" is sobering. People who are plugged-in to an authentic, loving small group are doing better at work, at home with the kids, in marriage, in their walk with Christ, and even in their finances. In fact, we found that people in *healthy* small groups scored higher on 53 out of 58 LifeSigns (91% of the items).

Let me first clarify what we mean by a "healthy" small group, versus an un-healthy group. While there are many characteristics of a vibrant group, the distinguishing characteristic we used is *relational depth*—the degree to which it's safe to deal with real life issues. The healthier the group, the more "real life" you're willing to tackle together.

LifeSigns data collected from thousands of people indicates that 48% are in some kind of small group; the remaining 52% are either looking for a group or just not interested.

CONVERSATION ONE – LIFE WITH PEOPLE

Of those who are in a small group, here's the breakdown: 60% are in healthy groups, 32% are in shallow groups where they don't feel connected, and 8% are in groups, but rarely attend.

"What's the point?" you ask, "I don't do statistics."

Here's the bottom line: People in a healthy small group are doing better than just about everyone else, in just about every area of life that we covered in LifeSigns (see below).

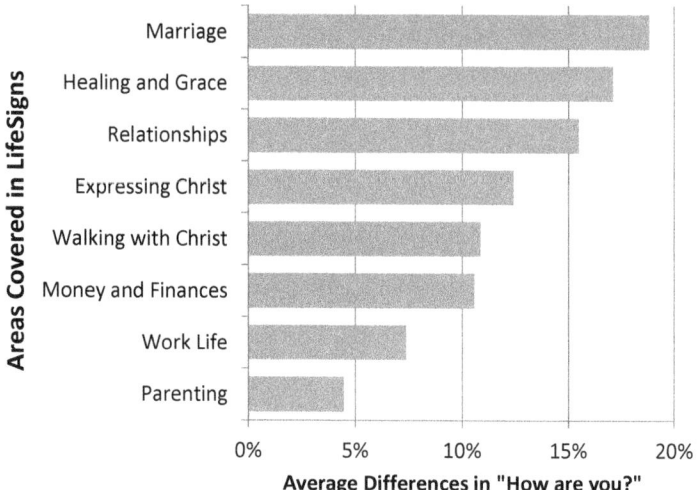

However, there's a wrinkle to this story: We found that being in a shallow group is worse for your spiritual health than being alone. People who said, "Yes I'm in a small group, but it's shallow, inconsistent, and superficial" are doing the *worst of anyone* in 17 of the LifeSigns items. The number one complaint from these folks is, "We rarely deal with the difficult issues of life." People in shallow small groups are hurting, but they're hiding. It's not safe, and they know it. Their LifeSigns scores are lower than for people who are not in *any* small group, and lower than those who only attend a small group infrequently.

Upon seeing this, one pastor concluded, "It looks like being fake is more dangerous than being alone."

Relationships are Essential for Growth

Intimate, authentic relationships are the fertile soil in which you'll grow. God uses these kinds of relationships to lift you up when you fall and to teach you how to love people through thick and thin. While solitude has its place, and we'll discuss it more in the next chapter, God never intended for you to go it alone. Whether you're the extroverted life of the party, or more an introvert, relationships with other believers are essential—not optional.

Life and Death in the Jungle

Think back for a moment to Forrest Gump caught in the fire fight in Vietnam.

As soon as Forrest realized that he was clear of enemy fire, he froze in his tracks and said, "I gotta find Bubba!" He turned and ran back into the smoke and chaos, only to discover other wounded members of his platoon along the way. So, one by one he carried his comrades to safety.

"I started to get scared that I might never find Bubba," he said.

Then, moments before an air-strike incinerated the jungle, ignoring the warnings of Lieutenant Dan, Forrest plunged head-first into enemy territory *yet again*. There is no better picture of friendship: Running back into the fire to save a friend.

Years ago, we'd show that six-minute clip from *Forrest Gump* to hundreds of men entering an intensive, nine-month discipleship program called Top Gun.[4] A lot can happen in nine months, and often less than half the guys in a group would graduate from the program. So, each year, I'd stand up and challenge our new recruits: *"Make the commitment right now.*

---

[4] Search YouTube for "Gump and Bubba in Vietnam" to see the clip. Just be aware, it's full of colorful language and may not be appropriate for kids.

Conversation One – Life with People

You're not going to leave anyone behind." We'd remind them that Forrest risked life and limb to find his friend Bubba, not because he was the designated leader of the platoon, not because he was some kind of superhero, but because he knew something terrible had happened to his friend.

Forrest had to find Bubba. *Nothing else mattered.*

Even though *Forrest Gump* is just a Hollywood movie, I get tears thinking about that kind of friendship. It's powerful and deeply moving, perhaps because it reminds us of our greatest need: someone to rescue us.

And someone has.

Jesus risked life and limb in order to have a relationship with you. He didn't just create the world, watch Adam and Eve fall into sin, and then shake His head in dismay from the safety of heaven's throne room.

Jesus came back for you.

The Bible tells us that Jesus personally led a search and rescue mission in order to, "seek and save that which was lost" (John 3:17). You see, He knew that something terrible had happened to you. You'd been lost deep in enemy territory. He knew that you'd been mortally wounded by sin, and nothing short of God's direct intervention could save you.

I know you've probably heard this passage from the book of John before but read it again. Slowly. *He's talking about you.* Jesus said, "Greater love has no one than this: to lay down one's life for one's friends…You did not choose me, but I chose you" (John 15:13, 16).

Jesus deliberately chose you. He wanted a relationship with you so badly, He was willing to be accused, tortured, and executed on the cross to get it. By laying down His life for you, Jesus provided the ultimate example of friendship under fire. He demonstrated His love for you, in that while you lay wounded and helpless in the jungle, He came back for you (Romans 5:8). *It cost him dearly, but He had to find you. Nothing else mattered.*

That, my friends, is friendship in action.

Here's the cool part of the story: Every day, you have an opportunity to do the same thing Jesus did. In the power of Christ, God can use you to help rescue the walking wounded all around you. Not just in your church group, but with your spouse, with your kids, with your neighbors, or even with someone you notice quietly weeping in their cubicle at work.

Do you know someone who is hurting, lost, or without hope? Then God has a search and rescue mission for you: "This is how we know what love is: Jesus Christ laid down his life for us. And we ought to lay down our lives for our brothers and sisters" (1 John 3:16).

You see, Jesus is still in the serious business of rescuing people from the clutches of the enemy.

And He'll use you to do it.

If you let Him.

Conversation One – Life with People

LifeSign #1: Trusting Others

Authenticity: Going deep in relationships and being able to talk about REAL LIFE (being yourself without having to fake it or pretend everything is fine, even if it's not)

Conversation Starters

What do you think?
1. What makes someone "safe?" What makes them "un-safe?"
2. How do you "self-protect" in relationships?
3. Think back: When you've had a deep, authentic relationship in the past, how did it happen? How did it develop?

Biblical Foundations

What does God say?
- "And let us consider how we may spur one another on toward love and good deeds, not giving up meeting together, as some are in the habit of doing, but encouraging one another—and all the more as you see the Day approaching." (Hebrews 10:24-25)
- "Finally, all of you, live in harmony with one another; be sympathetic, love as brothers, be compassionate and humble." (1 Peter 3:8)

Ideas for Growth

Okay, so now what?
- Commit to relationship with a small group of believers. This could be a community group, a one-on-one mentoring relationship, or a gathering of one or two close friends at Starbucks. Life is better together!
- Learn how to drop your mask and engage in authentic relationships in *True Faced* by Bill Thrall.
- Consider going through the excellent small group study *Authentic Relationships: Discover the Lost Art of One Anothering* by Wayne Jacobsen.

Your Next Step: _____
_____
_____

LIFESIGNS: HOW ARE YOU? REALLY.

LIFESIGN #2: LOVE AND ACCEPTANCE

Acceptance: When you've taken a risk to engage in a relationship, being LOVED and accepted by others (supported as a member of the family or a brother/sister in Christ, not judged or labeled)

CONVERSATION STARTERS

What do you think?
1. What kinds of labels, even if unspoken, do we sometimes put on people?
2. Jesus was criticized for spending time with certain kinds of people. Why?
3. How would people describe *you*? What kind of friend are you? (Ask the person across from you.)

BIBLICAL FOUNDATIONS

What does God say?
- "A friend loves at all times, and a brother is born for a time of adversity." (Proverbs 17:17)
- "Above all, love each other deeply, because love covers over a multitude of sins." (1 Peter 4:8)
- "Do not repay evil with evil or insult with insult, but with blessing, because to this you were called so that you may inherit a blessing." (1 Peter 3:9)

IDEAS FOR GROWTH

Okay, so now what?
- Check out *Grace Walk* by Steve McVey. Listen to the song *Come as You Are* by Jaci Valescez. Both vividly illustrate how the love of God as grace-based rather than shame-based. When you're grounded in God's grace, it will then overflow into your relationships with people.
- Write a note to your closest friends and/or family telling them what you love about them: "Dear Dad, here's what I love and appreciate about you..." As you love/accept them, they're more likely to love/accept you in return. Try it!

YOUR NEXT STEP: _____
_____
_____

CONVERSATION ONE – LIFE WITH PEOPLE

LifeSign #3: Talking about God's Word

Growth: Talking with friends about what you're LEARNING from Scripture (sharing new insights, exploring questions, finding practical applications from the Bible)

CONVERSATION STARTERS

What do you think?
1. In our current culture, is it considered "normal" to talk about the Bible with friends? Or is it politically incorrect?
2. What are the benefits of talking with friends about what you're learning from the Bible? How does it help you grow in Christ?

BIBLICAL FOUNDATIONS

What does God say?
- "All Scripture is God-breathed and is useful for teaching, rebuking, correcting and training in righteousness, so that the man of God may be thoroughly equipped for every good work." (2 Timothy 3:16-17)
- "Apply your heart to instruction and your ears to words of knowledge." (Proverbs 23:12)
- For more insight read 2 Timothy 3.

IDEAS FOR GROWTH

Okay, so now what?
- Join a small group of believers at your church. Most churches offer a wide variety of groups and classes on topics that impact your everyday life.
- Need a kick-start to get the most out of scripture? Work through *Living by the Book* by Howard Hendricks. The Bible will come alive in new ways.
- Blog about your insights from scripture and send the link to your friends. Pray for opportunities to discuss what you are learning from the Bible with people in your orbit. You'll both grow.

YOUR NEXT STEP: _____
_____
_____

LIFESIGNS: HOW ARE YOU? REALLY.

LIFESIGN #4: FORGIVENESS

Forgiving Others: When someone hurts you, choosing to let it go (making the first move, even if it's mostly another person's fault, forgiving rather than holding a grudge)

CONVERSATION STARTERS

What do you think?
1. What's the hardest part about "letting go" of a hurt caused by someone else?
2. What happens when small resentments are allowed to build up over time?
3. What if someone doesn't "deserve" to be forgiven? Then what?

BIBLICAL FOUNDATIONS

What does God say?
- "Be kind and compassionate to one another, forgiving each other, just as in Christ God forgave you." (Ephesians 4:32)
- "Then Peter came to Jesus and asked, 'Lord, how many times shall I forgive my brother when he sins against me? Up to seven times?' Jesus answered, 'I tell you, not seven times, but seventy-seven times.'" (Matthew 18:21-22)
- Also see Matthew chapters 18-22.

IDEAS FOR GROWTH

Okay, so now what?
- Work through *The Peacemaker* book by Ken Sande and/or small group DVD study.
- To work on reconciliation in your marriage: read and put into practice the book, *Love and Respect* by Emerson Eggerichs.

YOUR NEXT STEP: _____
_____
_____

Conversation One – Life with People

LifeSign #5: Reaching Out

New Friendships: Reaching out to INITIATE relationships with people who don't know Christ or go to church (inviting someone to lunch or coffee, to see a game, to visit church)

Conversation Starters

What do you think?
1. Why bother? Seriously, you're really busy. Why reach out to someone who may not go to church or know Jesus?
2. Exactly HOW do you initiate a new relationship with someone?
3. When you've tried to reach out, how do people typically respond?

Biblical Foundations

What does God say?
- "To the weak I became weak, to win the weak. I have become all things to all men so that by all possible means I might save some." (1 Corinthians 9:22)
- "Therefore, go and make disciples of all nations, baptizing them in the name of the Father and of the Son and of the Holy Spirit, and teaching them to obey everything I have commanded you." (Matthew 28:19-20)

Ideas for Growth

Okay, so now what?
- Go on prayer walks through the neighborhood or area of town you are interested in engaging. Pray that you will be alert for opportunities the Holy Spirit provides for engaging with the people.
- Read *Coffee Shop Conversations: Making the Most of Spiritual Small Talk* by Dale Fincher or *Walk Across the Room* by Bill Hybels for inspiration in sharing the hope that you have in Jesus.

Your Next Step: _____
_____
_____

LifeSigns: How are you? Really.

LifeSign #6: Accountability

Accountability: Maintaining a healthy level of ACCOUNTABILITY with a friend (being honest with someone who asks hard questions, answering fully and truthfully)

Conversation Starters

What do you think?
1. What does it really mean to "be accountable" with someone?
2. What are the benefits? What are the drawbacks?
3. How do you balance accountability with grace?

Biblical Foundations

What does God say?
- "As iron sharpens iron, so one person sharpens another." (Proverbs 27:17)
- "Therefore, confess your sins to each other and pray for each other so that you may be healed. The prayer of a righteous person is powerful and effective." (James 5:16) For context read James 5.
- "So then, each of us will give an account of ourselves to God." (Romans 14:12)

Ideas for Growth

Okay, so now what?
- You're not really accountable to another person, you're accountable to Christ. But a friend can help remind you of that fact. Consider asking someone to coffee, bring your LifeSigns profile, and dive into a conversation about "how you are...really."
- Read and work through *Soul Revolution* by John Burke. Choose a "running partner" (he will define what that is) and walk through the 60/60 challenge he suggests.

Your Next Step: _____
_____
_____

Conversation One – Life with People

LifeSign #7: Having a "Best Friend"

Best Friend: Not just a buddy or social media contact, but someone you've TRUSTED with your struggles and secrets (you could call them at midnight, honestly share, get encouragement and prayer)

CONVERSATION STARTERS

What do you think?
1. What's the difference between an "acquaintance" and a "best friend?"
2. Did Jesus have any best friends?
3. How long does it take to build a deep friendship? Can you share a personal example of a BFF?

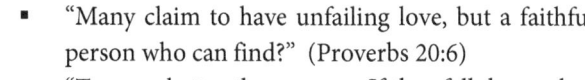

BIBLICAL FOUNDATIONS

What does God say?
- "Many claim to have unfailing love, but a faithful person who can find?" (Proverbs 20:6)
- "Two are better than one . . . If they fall down, they can help each other up. But pity those who fall and have no one to help them up! . . . Though one may be overpowered, two can defend themselves." (Ecclesiastes 4:9-12)
- "A man of many companions may come to ruin, but there is a friend who sticks closer than a brother." (Proverbs 18:24)

IDEAS FOR GROWTH

Okay, so now what?
- Deep friendships usually don't just happen—they are carefully cultivated over the years. If you lack this kind of a friend, pray that you will see someone God has put in your path, then take the initiative.
- Make the first move, invite people out for a coffee or meal or have them over to your home. Remember that the relationship is important, not the surroundings.

YOUR NEXT STEP: _____
_____
_____

LifeSigns: How are you? Really.

LifeSign #8: Connecting in a Small Group

Are you actively participating in a small group of some kind at church? (i.e., a community group, Bible study, serving group, etc.)

Conversation Starters

What do you think?
1. Have you ever been in an intimate, healthy small group? (i.e., could be any kind of group: sports, church, work, school, club, etc.)
2. What's your definition of a "healthy small group?" What's it like?
3. What are the pros/cons of investing yourself in a small group?

Biblical Foundations

What does God say?
- "If we walk in the light, as he is in the light, we have fellowship with one another, and the blood of Jesus, his Son, purifies us from all sin." (1 John 1:7)
- "They devoted themselves to the apostles' teaching and to the fellowship, to the breaking of bread and to prayer...Selling their possessions and goods, they gave to anyone as he had need...They broke bread in their homes and ate together with glad and sincere hearts, praising God...And the Lord added to their number daily those who were being saved." (Acts 2:42-47 NIV). Also read Acts 2.

Ideas for Growth

Okay, so now what?
- No group is perfect. Looking for a small group is not like shopping for a shiny new car, it's more like building a house together: noisy, messy, slow, and never quite finished. You get to enjoy the process, not just the end product.
- Get involved in serving with other Christians. Relationships develop as you do ministry together.

Your Next Step: _____
_____
_____

Conversation Two

LIFE WITH JESUS

"It's not crazy. It's a Father-son project."

Let's go back to the day I finally told my mom that I'd signed up to do the Ironman triathlon.

"What's that?" she asked suspiciously.

I explained that an official Ironman triathlon consists of a 2.4-mile ocean swim, a 112-mile bike, followed by a full marathon of 26.2 miles. That's a total of 140.6 miles—all in the same day.
"Oh yeah," I added, "and I have to finish before midnight."
There was a moment of awkward silence. Mom looked me square in the eye and said, *"That's crazy."*

Conversation Two – Life with Jesus

In many ways, Mom is right. Training for an Ironman is like having a second full-time job with bizarre hours, horrible working conditions, and an embarrassing uniform. Few of us look good in a speedo or spandex bike shorts, me included.

When you're not busy swimming, biking, and running, you're fussing over your nutrition, equipment, and training plan. What's worse, as the calendar counts down to race day, you start to feel like a man on death row. There's this nagging fear that you're probably going to die a slow, painful death before you reach the finish line.

So, what on earth could possess an otherwise rational person to do something so strenuous and, quite frankly, unnecessary?

A "Father-Son Project"

Growing up, I loved building stuff in the garage with my dad. Dad is a brilliant mechanical engineer with a tool for every job. Back then, he was always eager to get his hands dirty building a go-cart, fixing a bicycle, or erecting a fort that was the envy of the neighborhood. We even got him a t-shirt that says, "My father can fix anything."

At some point in every father-son project, there is a moment of truth. The son strips the threads on a bolt, bloodies a knuckle, and throws up his hands, and yells, "Daaaad! I can't do this!" The son's brow is furrowed; hot tears run down his grease stained cheeks. Stick around long enough and you'll eventually hear the son say, "I've had it Dad. I quit!"

That is a magical moment.

As my friend Paul Miller says, "When you've reached the end of yourself, that's a good place to be." He's right. The end of yourself is where your relationship with Christ becomes real. It's where life-lessons are learned, character is developed, and you finally and fully experience God's grace. That's why James talks about considering it "pure joy" when you encounter trials and tribulations (James 1:2-4). It sounds crazy, but according to James, it's how God makes us "perfect and complete, lacking in nothing." The apostle Paul goes even further and says you can actually "exult in tribulations," knowing that you won't be disappointed because, "God's love has been poured out into our hearts through the Holy Spirit, who has been given to us." (Romans 5:3-5). In light of this truth, maybe we should print some t-shirts that say, "My heavenly Father can fix anything."

So, let me ask: *Have you ever reached the end of yourself?*

You don't have to experience dehydration and sunstroke 100 miles into an Ironman bike to find it. The end of yourself may come at 9:30 on a Tuesday night when you're exhausted, the kids are fighting, the laundry is piled high, and your spouse is missing in action. The end of yourself can be something as mundane as facing another day in a dead-end job, or as terrifying as hearing the doctor say, "I'm very sorry, it's malignant."

Here's the point. *Your whole life is essentially a "father-son project." Everything.* Or if you prefer, your whole life is essentially a father-daughter project. You're not supposed to be able to do it on your own. That's why Jesus put it so bluntly, "Apart from Me, you can do nothing" (John 15:4).

Nothing? Really?

John Eldredge explains it this way, "Jesus is not berating us or mocking us or even saying it with a sigh, all the while thinking, 'I wish they'd pull it together and stop needing me so much.' Not at all. We are made to depend on God; we are made for union with him and nothing about us works right without it."[5]

GETTING PRACTICAL: A CONSTANT CONVERSATION

In my opinion, one of the most unreasonable verses in the Bible is also one of the shortest: "Pray continually." Another version says, "Pray without ceasing" (1 Thessalonians 5:17).

Let me get this straight. I'm supposed to talk to God continually—without stopping? You can't be serious. You have

---

[5] John Eldredge, *Wild at Heart* (Thomas Nelson, Inc., Nashville, Tennessee, 2001), p. 121.

Conversation Two – Life with Jesus

no idea how complex and demanding my day is at work, how my schedule is jammed from dawn to dusk. I'm lucky to squeeze in a quick devotional before bed.

Have you ever felt this way?

Please know that it's not only possible to "pray without ceasing," but I've discovered it's the very essence of Life with Jesus. It's how your relationship with Jesus moves beyond a Sunday ritual and into your daily, chaos-filled life. Here's how it happened for me.

As I spent 12 months training for my first Ironman back in 2003, all those long hours spent swimming, biking, and running opened the door to a vibrant new world in my relationship with Christ. Before, I'd only tasted this kind of intimacy with Jesus at a retreat, conference, or on a Sunday morning. But all those intimidating, lonely workouts became the perfect opportunity for "a long conversation" with my heavenly Father.

And we talked about everything.

At first, it was hard to focus, as I dodged potholes and pick-up trucks on my bike. Sometimes I'd tape an index card to my handlebars with topics for our conversation. Often, I'd use the A-C-T-S method of prayer to lend some structure, and it worked amazingly well. On a six-hour training ride, I'd spend the first hour praising Him for being so awesome (Adoration), the second hour sharing my struggles (Confession), the third hour thanking Him for all the good stuff in my life (Thanksgiving), and the fourth asking for His grace and help in time of need (Supplication). Sometimes we'd dig deeply into a bit of scripture I'd memorized. But most of the time, we were just a Father and son, out there doing something fun and difficult *together*.

As the hours of effort passed, the accumulated fatigue and pain would strip away the crust on my heart, leaving me emotionally raw and desperate before Him. To be honest, the fifth and sixth hours of monster 120-mile training rides were less about deep theological conversation and more about simply clinging to my Daddy for courage. Even as I share this story with you, tears fill my eyes and splash onto the keyboard, just remembering all those special moments, out on the open road with Him. And that's how our father-son project was born.

Then something amazing happened.

The conversation did not stop when the workout was over. I soon realized that we were talking all the time: in the shower, in the car, during meetings, mowing the lawn, cooking dinner. And through that constant conversation, I discovered a whole new level of intimacy with my Dad. Our relationship blossomed, becoming real and tangible like never before. I started to relate to some of those wild Psalms that capture David's passionate conversations with God. They didn't seem so wild after all.

Stop and consider: *How often do you really talk with Him?* God longs to connect with you personally, intimately. Many times, and in various ways, the Bible says that if you seek God with all your heart, you will find Him (see Jeremiah 29:13). Sure, you may relate to God differently than I do, but when you share your heart with Him, He will surprise you.

That's why the "Life with Jesus" section of LifeSigns is focused on the practical, intimate parts of your everyday relationship with Jesus. We asked how frequently you are deeply connecting with Him, hearing Him speak through the Bible, changing direction when He gives you a nudge, and depending on His grace when you struggle. Yes, of course you should have a quiet time and read your Bible, but your relationship with Christ is so much bigger and messier than that.

At least it should be.

THE MOST IMPORTANT QUESTION OF ALL: WHO ARE YOU? REALLY.

LifeSigns is mostly about your *condition* in Christ, which is why we ask, "How are you?" But what about your *position* in Christ? That is, "Who are you?" Usually, our identity is defined by our career, "I'm a software developer," by our family role, "I'm a mother of two," or by our accomplishments. All those things accurately describe what you *do*, but they're not who you *are*. So, let me ask, what is your true identity? Your answer to that question is critical. It reveals what you believe and ultimately, how you live.

I didn't do an Ironman to become a *different* person, I did it to discover a *new person*. Let me explain.

If you watch NBC's Emmy Award-winning coverage of the Ironman World Championship in Kona, Hawaii, you'll hear first timers talk in reverent tones about becoming an Ironman. You'll see people running (or crawling) down the final stretch to cross the finish line, and you'll hear the announcer proclaim, "Jason Smith, you are an IRONMAN!" You'll see tears of joy and wonder, hugs, and high-fives. Finishers will gush about how they've gained a new sense of identity and personal worth that can never be taken away from them. Even the ladies will proudly proclaim, "I'm an Ironman!" Heck, some of my training buddies even got an Ironman tattoo. They'll never be the same!

I'm afraid they're going to be disappointed.

It takes about a week. The warm glow of victory fades just as quickly as those sore muscles. You put your shiny finisher's medal on the shelf and go back to work. You soon discover a critical question remains unanswered: "Who am I? Really." In fact, I've read serious articles written by experts about how to cope with "Post Ironman Depression." Most Ironman finishers I know feel empty and unfulfilled once the race is over, perhaps because they realize that nothing has really changed.

When we construct our identity based on our work, family, or achievements, there remains a void in every person's heart. It's an emptiness that can never be filled with a college degree or a career, with a nice home and nice things, or even with a loving spouse and beautiful children. (Though all those things are very good indeed.)

Here's the truth: "If anyone is in Christ, he or she is a new person; the old things have passed away and a new life has come"

LifeSigns: How are you? Really.

(2 Corinthians 5:17). The unexpected result of all those long conversations with God while swimming, biking, and running was the discovery of *who I really am* in His eyes. Yes, crossing the Ironman finish line was a major accomplishment, *but discovering my true life in Christ was the real reward.* My true identity in Christ is the finisher's medal I wear proudly around my neck all the days of my life. And I'm never taking it off.

Major Ian Thomas put it this way, "Christ gave His life *for you*, so he could give His life *to you*, so he could live His life *through you*."

It's kind of hard to swallow, given our culture: Your true significance and worth are defined by what Jesus accomplished, not by anything you've accomplished. By dying on the cross for you, He proved you're worth everything to Him. But He didn't stop at death; He rose from the grave and lives today. As you surrender yourself to Him, at the moment that you trust Jesus for salvation, He gives you a new identity and adopts you into His family. That is where your significance comes from.

I can't say it any better than my pastor, Pete Briscoe: "You see, the Bible teaches us that there is an irreversible, supernatural transformation that takes place the moment that we put our trust in Christ. We are radically changed for all of eternity and that radical, irreversible transformation can never be lost. We are now children of God, we are in Christ, and we are in union with Him."

Maybe it's time for a "long conversation" with your Father about *who* you are in Christ. Really.

Conversation Starters

Instructions: On page four of your LifeSigns Growth Plan, it shows your top priority from the Life with Jesus section. In the pages that follow, you'll find conversation starters, scriptures, and resources for each topic.

Just flip to the page with the LifeSign that interests you, and dive into a candid conversation about who you are. Really.

Conversation Two – Life with Jesus

LifeSign #1: Assurance of Salvation

Salvation: Reaching a point where you're CERTAIN you've been restored to a right relationship with God, through His son Jesus Christ – and that you're 100% forgiven and accepted

CONVERSATION STARTERS

What do you think?
1. Do you believe that it's even possible to be 100% certain of your salvation? Or is there always going to be some room for doubt?
2. Where are you on the journey to discovering how to have a relationship with Jesus?

What does God say?

BIBLICAL FOUNDATIONS

- "God has given us eternal life, and this life is in his Son. He who has the Son has life... I write these things to you who believe in the name of the Son of God, so that you may know that you have eternal life." (I John 5:11-13)
- "For all have sinned and fall short of the glory of God... justified freely by His grace through the redemption that came by Jesus Christ." (Romans 3:23-24)

Okay, so now what?

IDEAS FOR GROWTH

- Learn how to begin a relationship with Jesus. In just eight minutes, pastor Pete Briscoe will walk you through the process and answer questions you may have. Go to vimeo.com/26888450 to watch the video. Be sure to share your decision to trust Christ with a friend or pastor.
- Here are two more fantastic web sites that answer questions about the gospel and salvation. Check out www.NeedHim.com or www.IamSecond.com.

Your Next Step: _____
_____
_____

LifeSigns: How are you? Really.

LifeSign #2: Intimacy with Christ

Intimacy with Christ: On any given day, having an INTIMATE encounter with Jesus (being fully aware of God's presence, hearing His voice, experiencing His peace)

Conversation Starters

What do you think?
1. Describe a time when you felt totally connected with God. How did it happen?
2. On an everyday basis, how do you connect with God the best? (e.g., worship music or during a workout, alone in your room or in a crowded coffee shop?)

Biblical Foundations

What does God say?
- "Remain in me, and I will remain in you. No branch can bear fruit by itself...unless you remain in me" (John 15:4). Read all of John 15 for context.
- "Let us draw near to God with a sincere heart and with the full assurance that faith brings, having our hearts sprinkled to cleanse us from a guilty conscience." (Hebrews 10:22)
- "But blessed is the man who trusts in the Lord, whose confidence is in him. He will be like a tree planted by the water that sends out its roots by the stream. It does not fear when heat comes...and never fails to bear fruit." (Jeremiah 17:7-8)

Ideas for Growth

Okay, so now what?
- This book is awesome: *Sacred Pathways: Discover Your Soul's Path to God* by Gary Thomas.
- Another great book is *The Life You've Always Wanted* by John Ortberg.
- Ask a friend how they connect with Christ.

Your Next Step: _____
_____
_____

Conversation Two – Life with Jesus

LifeSign #3: Authentic Worship

Group Worship: Fully ENGAGING with and FOCUSING on Christ during Sunday services (through the music, prayer, preaching)

Conversation Starters

What do you think?
1. How would you define "authentic worship?"
2. What keeps you from fully engaging and worshipping God? Not just at a church service. How can you become totally focused on Him and His awesomeness?

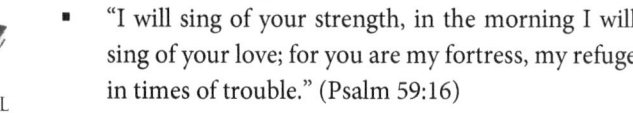
Biblical Foundations

What does God say?
- "I will sing of your strength, in the morning I will sing of your love; for you are my fortress, my refuge in times of trouble." (Psalm 59:16)
- "Come near to God and he will come near to you." (James 4:8)
- "Praise the Lord. Praise God in his sanctuary; praise him in his mighty heavens. Praise him for his acts of power; praise him for his surpassing greatness...praise him with timbrel and dancing... Let everything that has breath praise the Lord." (Psalm 150)

Ideas for Growth

Okay, so now what?
- As you sing or listen to the music during the corporate worship at church, really focus on the words and lyrics. The songs are carefully selected to communicate a message. What is it?
- Stretch yourself in expressions of worship. Sometimes the lyrics instruct the worshipper to raise hands or close eyes or bow down. Consider physically expressing yourself in these ways.

Your Next Step: _____
_____
_____

LifeSigns: How are you? Really.

LifeSign #4: Learning from the Bible

Learning Truth: Hearing God speak to you clearly THROUGH the Bible (by studying Scripture on your own, in a small group, by hearing a sermon)

Conversation Starters

What do you think?
1. Hebrews 4 says God's word is "living and active." What does that mean?
2. Share one example, or verse, God has used to speak very clearly to you. What was the message?

Biblical Foundations

What does God say?
- "For the word of God is alive and active. Sharper than any double-edged sword, it penetrates even to dividing soul and spirit, joints and marrow; it judges the thoughts and attitudes of the heart." (Hebrews 4:12)
- "I seek you with all my heart; do not let me stray from your commands. I have hidden your word in my heart that I might not sin against you." (Psalms 119:10)

Ideas for Growth

Okay, so now what?
- This is one of the most helpful resources: *Living by the Book Workbook: The Art and Science of Reading the Bible* by Howard and William Hendricks.
- Pick up a copy of *Read the Bible for Life: Your Guide to Understanding & Living God's Word* by George H. Guthrie.

Your Next Step: _____
_____
_____

Conversation Two – Life with Jesus

LifeSign #5: Applying the Bible to Life

Application: Finding ways to practically APPLY the principles and truths from the Bible in your everyday life (at home, at work, with your kids, in your personal life)

Conversation Starters

What do you think?
1. Can you apply God's word without God?
2. Share a specific verse that you'd really like to apply in your everyday life.
3. When it comes to putting it into action, what is God's role, and what's your role? Specifically.

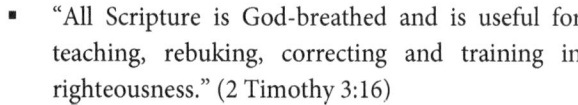
Biblical Foundations

What does God say?
- "All Scripture is God-breathed and is useful for teaching, rebuking, correcting and training in righteousness." (2 Timothy 3:16)
- "Do not merely listen to the word...Do what it says. Anyone who listens to the word but does not do what it says is like a man who looks at his face in a mirror and, after looking at himself, goes away and immediately forgets what he looks like. But the man who looks intently into the perfect law that gives freedom... he will be blessed in what he does." (James 1:22-25) For context read James 1 and 2.

Ideas for Growth

Okay, so now what?
- Remember: The bible is not about rules, it's about a relationship. Read Psalm 119. How many different ways do you find the Psalmist saying that he applies the Word of God daily to his life?
- Consider reading *Bible Study Methods* by Rick Warren. Focus on the first chapter on the *Devotional Method*.

Your Next Step: _____
_____
_____

LifeSigns: How are you? Really.

LifeSign #6: Responding to God's Leading

Surrender: Responding by faith when God prompts you to CHANGE direction in your life (hearing God's voice and responding to Him – whether the change is large or small)

Conversation Starters

What do you think?
1. How does God "speak" to us?
2. Share one example of how God has prompted you to "change direction" in your life. What was the message?
3. How long did it take you to respond? Why?

Biblical Foundations

What does God say?
- "Today, if only you would hear his voice, do not harden your hearts…" (Psalm 95:7-8)
- "The gatekeeper opens the gate for him, and the sheep listen to his voice. He calls his own sheep by name and leads them out. When he has brought out all his own, he goes on ahead of them, and his sheep follow him because they know his voice. But they will never follow a stranger; in fact, they will run away from him because they do not recognize a stranger's voice." (Jesus in John 10:3-5)

Ideas for Growth

Okay, so now what?
- This book has proven tremendously helpful in learning to listen and follow God's voice: *The Power of a Whisper: Hearing God.*
- For inspiration read *Fresh Wind, Fresh Fire* by Jim Cymbala, or *E.M. Bounds on Prayer* by E.M. Bounds.

Your Next Step: _____
_____
_____

Conversation Two – Life with Jesus

LifeSign #7: Depending on Christ

Living by Faith: When facing difficulties, depending on Christ and His strength – rather than your own strength (by stepping out in faith, trying something new, relying on the Spirit's power)

Conversation Starters

What do you think?
1. Have you ever reached the "end of yourself?"
2. What did you do? Where was God in the mix?
3. Share one area of your life where it's difficult to trust God right now. Pray for each other.

Biblical Foundations

What does God say?
- "Such confidence we have through Christ toward God. Not that we are adequate in ourselves to consider anything as coming from ourselves, but our adequacy is from God." (2 Corinthians 3:4-5)
- "Trust in the Lord with all your heart and lean not on your own understanding; in all your ways acknowledge him, and he will make your paths straight." (Proverbs 3:5-6)
- "Going a little farther, he [Jesus] fell with his face to the ground and prayed, 'My Father, if it is possible, may this cup be taken from me. Yet not as I will, but as you will.'" (Matthew 26:29). For context, read Matthew 26.

Ideas for Growth

Okay, so now what?
- It all comes down to this: Do you really believe that God is good—even if circumstances are bad? If you're struggling, the number one resource we recommend is *Grace Walk* by Steve McVey.
- Many people have been helped by reading the book *Broken Down House* by Paul David Tripp.

Your Next Step: _____
_____
_____

Conversation Three

Life with Purpose

"For Christ's love compels us."
- 2 Corinthians 5:14

Y ou see, I just couldn't help it.

When I first became a Christian half-way through my freshman year of college, a radical transformation swept through my world. In just one semester, I went from chasing women and racing cars, to pursing Christ with the same zeal. Pretty soon, I had a new set of friends, who knew how to have fun sober, a new set of priorities, and a whole new direction in life. My grades even improved—a miracle in itself.

With that first summer break came the 12-hour drive from Lubbock back home to Houston. Somewhere north of Abilene, in

CONVERSATION THREE – LIFE WITH PURPOSE

the middle of nowhere, my conversation with God reached a fever pitch: "Lord I love you! Take my life, I'm all yours." At that very moment, in the distance, I see a handful of people working in the rows of a vast cotton field.

"Lord do *those* people know you?" I asked.

One quick U-turn and one quick prayer later, I'm parked alongside the highway, with the field stretching into the horizon. The workers stop and regard me with puzzled expressions as I scramble across the dusty furrows.

"Hi there. Um, I just wanted to ask you guys something," I say. Uh-oh. "You don't speak English?"

It doesn't matter, I hand them each a gospel tract and tell them, with frantic and incomprehensible gestures, that God above loves them and sent His son to the cross for them. They smile and nod. I smile back. Not knowing what to do next, we all shake hands and I scramble back across the field to my car.

Like I said, I just couldn't help it.

A few hours later, in the small town of Giddings, I stop at a local bar to talk with three bewildered cowboys nursing their beers about knowing God. Later outside Austin, I visit a Psychic who informs me that her powers do, in fact, come from God, as she ushers me out of her shop and onto the sidewalk. At a gas station in Brenham, I fervently pray from the parking lot as I watch the clerk inside read the little booklet I'd given him. Needless to say, it was an interesting trip.

During that first summer as a Christian, most of my high-school drinking buddies, two old girlfriends, and a kid I met fishing on a dock all accepted Christ. One afternoon we had a Bible study by the pool. We studied John 3:16, "For God so loved the world…" Why? Because it was the only verse I knew. My best friend David said "Yes" to Jesus that day.

Over the next four years, I lived in a non air-conditioned dorm on campus just to build relationships with guys who needed Christ. It was great. One night after a bible study in my room, we baptized half-a-dozen guys in the fountain at the main entrance of the university, keeping a lookout for the campus police, who probably would not understand. One time, I even stood outside the student union and preached to a crowd of about six people.

All these years later, *something has changed.*

Today, if I'm honest with you, I rarely make an effort to talk with people about how to begin a relationship with Jesus, except for our kids, of course. So, what happened? Well, there's been marriage and graduate school, a real corporate job, a mortgage, two kids, three dogs, and everything that comes with a busy life in Dallas, Texas. But that doesn't really explain it, does it?

Over the years, I think the sparkle and wonder of my new life in Christ has faded to familiarity, and with it, all those spontaneous conversations about spiritual things. I go weeks or months without even *thinking about people* who are far from God. Yes, I've got some guilt about that. Can you relate?

What drives you? Guilt or Grace?

I have two otherwise delightful children who, like most kids, will seldom eat a green vegetable or share a toy of their own free will. I read somewhere that yelling commands from the couch is a poor parenting strategy. So, I'm forced to deliver a vivid description of starving people in Africa, along with each serving of broccoli, or a sobering reminder that Jesus gave His life for them—so they can darn well share the TV remote.

I think it worked exactly once.

Unfortunately, I've seen frustrated pastors do exactly the same thing. It's not surprising. Church leaders must constantly find new ways to lift us from our pews and deploy us into noble and needed ministry. Guilt and shame will work—maybe once. But then what?

Try this: *The outrageous love of Christ.*

In the first century, people in the Corinthian church began to question the apostle Paul's true motives. Some even suggested that he was "out of his mind." So, Paul sent them a long,

Conversation Three – Life with Purpose

passionate letter to explain what was really happening. He wrote, "Christ's love *compels* me." Another translation says, "the love of Christ *controls* me." Paul is using the heavy-duty Greek word, "sunecho," that loses some of its punch when translated into the more civilized English word "compel." The original word literally means to be gripped, pressed, and besieged on every side by a force more powerful than yourself. In this case, Paul is saying, "Guys, you just don't understand what drives me. *I'm completely overwhelmed by the love of Christ.*"

In other words, he just couldn't help it.

Since God is supremely powerful, think of all the ways He could grab your attention and motivate you: earthquakes and lightning bolts, plague and pestilence, threats of punishment, or even a voice thundering from the sky. No, God doesn't use any of these methods to compel us. But then...how?

He uses Grace.

The reason grace is such a powerful force is revealed in the very next verse Paul wrote to the Corinthians: "Christ's love compels us, because we are convinced that one died for all, and therefore all died. And he died for all..." Are you ready for this? "...that those who live *should no longer live for themselves but for him who died for them and was raised again*" (2 Corinthians 5:13-15).

Paul is speaking from deep, personal experience. Before surrendering his life to Christ, Paul hunted down Christians, put them in jail, and even had some of them killed. This arrogant, murderous man, this persecutor of Christ himself, was radically redeemed by a grace that defied all human reason. Paul's enemy had swept him away in a flood of mercy. What drove the apostle Paul to the ends of the earth? Grace. What stoked the fires of his passion to burn white-hot, year after year, even in the face of horrendous trials and hardships? Grace! Why would Paul risk his life just to tell people about Jesus? Grace!

Through it all, I think Paul never got over God's extravagant gift of grace—something he didn't deserve, desperately needed, and could never repay. So much so he said, "I am *compelled* to preach," there's that word compelled again, "woe to me if I do not preach the gospel!" (1 Corinthians 9:16).

It's easy to intellectually grasp why we "should no longer live for ourselves" in light of Christ's love, but sometimes in the middle of my busy, messy life, I just don't feel very "compelled" to do much of anything for God.

If you're in the same boat, keep reading.

How God Changes You: Fruits and Roots

Images of planting, watering, pruning, and harvesting are used in scripture to help illustrate how you grow in Christ. For example, Jesus said, "This is to my Father's glory, that you bear much fruit" (John 15:8). But when your LifeSigns uncovers a gap between your beliefs and behaviors, between your good intentions and daily actions, it's easy to get discouraged. You may be tempted to draw up a spiritual self-improvement program and get busy "living for Jesus."

Don't do it. That's not how it works.

Yes, spiritual disciplines like praying and studying scripture are important, but those alone don't cause your growth. Paul explains it this way, "For God is working in you, giving you the *desire* and the *power* to do what pleases him." (Philippians 2:13). Notice who is doing the work: God is the one "working in you." And notice how he does it: God changes your heart (desire) and gives you the strength (power) to live differently.

So how, exactly, does God *cause* you to grow?

The idea of "fruits and roots" isn't new. I'll let Jesus explain: "No good tree bears bad fruit, nor does a bad tree bear good fruit. Each tree is recognized by its own fruit…A good man brings good things out of the good stored up in his heart, and an evil man brings evil things out of the evil stored up in his heart. What you say flows from what is in your heart." (Luke 6:43-45).

Notice it all starts with your heart. As you cooperate with the God's work, He changes you from the inside out: a new awareness takes root, your attitudes change, your abilities blossom, new behaviors sprout, and ultimately your life bears good fruit (see graphic). We grow from the inside out, from roots to fruits:

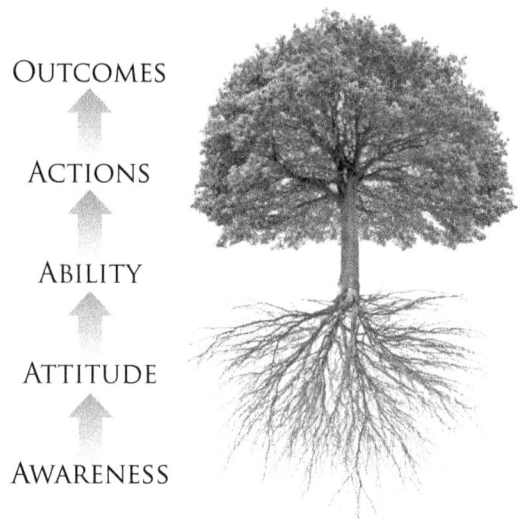

OUTCOMES

ACTIONS

ABILITY

ATTITUDE

AWARENESS

This process, while probably not as tidy as our lovely graphic suggests, is where to see God at work in your life. Before you discuss your LifeSigns results from this section with a friend, let's first briefly consider how the "compelling love of Christ" looks in action, starting with your roots and ending with your fruits.

COMPELLED BY GRACE – A NEW AWARENESS

Do you have new eyeballs?

One of the first steps in trusting Christ as your savior is gaining a new awareness of your true spiritual condition. "Wow," you say, "I'm lost, and He wants me back." But God doesn't stop there. When He takes up residence in your heart, the Spirit begins to reveal the world around you from his perspective, and you experience first-hand how "the Lord opens the eyes of the blind" (Psalm 146:8).

When an atheist named C.S. Lewis finally accepted Christ, he got a new pair of eyes—and he couldn't believe what he saw. Everyday people were cast in a vivid new, eternal light:

> *Remember that the dullest and most uninteresting person you talk to may one day be a creature which, if you saw it now, you would be strongly tempted to worship, or a horror and a corruption such as you now meet, only in a nightmare. There are no ordinary people. You have never talked to a mere mortal. Nations, cultures, arts, civilization—these are mortal, and their life is to ours as the life of a gnat. But it is immortals whom we joke with, work with, marry, snub, and exploit—immortal horrors or everlasting splendours.*[6]

Let that soak in. *There are no ordinary people.* All of us are destined, according to scripture, for one of two eternities: immortal horrors or everlasting splendours. That may sound politically incorrect, but it's also an accurate description of our spiritual condition.

The Apostle Paul knew only God could provide this kind of new awareness. That's why he prayed, "that your hearts will be flooded with light so that you can understand the confident hope he has given to those he called—his holy people who are his rich and glorious inheritance. I also pray that you will understand the incredible greatness of God's power for us who believe him." (Ephesians 1:18-19). That's a mouthful. Paul wanted people to see a new reality: you have hope, you are holy, and you have God's power. Why does it matter?

---

[6] C.S. Lewis, *The Weight of Glory* (Harper Collins, New York, New York, 2001), pp. 45-46

If you've trusted Jesus, your hope for the future is totally secure. The more fully you grasp the magnitude of your sin and the riches of His grace and love, the more aware you'll become of people who face a horrible future without Christ. What's worse, every day you're surrounded by people who are oblivious to their spiritual poverty and unaware of God's abundant love.

Their ship is sinking, *and they don't even know it.*

That can really start to "bother" you, if you let it. And that's a good sign.

COMPELLED BY GRACE – NEW ATTITUDES

I listened patiently for over an hour as a new Christian friend sat on my sidewalk detailing all the "big issues" in her life. Each sentence began with, "I'm just so…" and left me feeling more frustrated. When I finally realized that this self-absorbed exercise was getting us nowhere, I said, "Come on, I want to show you something."

In those days, the largest honky-tonk for hundreds of miles around was called Midnight Rodeo. With room for well over a thousand people, it had acres of dance floor, six bars, pulsating lights and loud music. Before we went in, I gave my friend a simple assignment: "I want you to look at people, look at their faces, and ask yourself this question: Where are they going? Not just tonight, but for eternity."

We breezed through the front door without paying a cover charge and were hardly noticed by the distracted bouncers. Now I've spent plenty of time in noisy nightclubs over the years, but when you're saved and sober, it's a completely different experience.

As you'd expect, we saw people dancing, yelling, and spilling beer on the floor. But one young lady caught our attention. She was drunk as a skunk and throwing herself at multiple men. The nearest guy propping her up had a menacing look, his hands wandering freely as he exchanged knowing nods with his buddies. We stopped. "Look at her long and hard," I said through the din. "Where do you think she's headed?"

For ten long minutes, we stood and watched helplessly from across the room, reminded that God was there, watching his daughter too. It was utterly heartbreaking.

After a while longer, we retreated to the fresh air of the parking lot to debrief and pray. The very next day, a story on the front page of the local newspaper helped to explain why the club staff seemed so distracted when we entered at about 10:30 PM.

The paramedics had just left.

Evidently a different woman had passed out in a bathroom stall, was found by her friends, and rushed to the hospital. She was pronounced dead upon arrival.

That day, my friend's attitude began to change about her "big issues" and her identity in Christ. Years later she attended seminary, become a licensed counselor, and spent the next ten years working with addicts. Christ had completely transformed her attitude—and the trajectory of her life in the process.

Compelled by Grace – a Surprise from the LifeSigns Data

We wondered what's so different about people who have a "heart for the lost." You may remember the LifeSigns question, it reads: "How often are you 'disturbed' by the thought of those who don't know Christ? (i.e., seeing people in light of eternity, as God sees them – rather than just as they exist today)."

Out of 55 different factors, the number one difference among those who "frequently" or "consistently" have a heart for the lost is *not* Bible study, *not* small group attendance, *not* serving in the church, or even being willing to reach out to strangers.

The single biggest difference is *daily intimacy with Christ.*

CONVERSATION THREE – LIFE WITH PURPOSE

Here's the LifeSigns question verbatim: "On a daily basis, how often do you experience an intimate connection with Christ? (i.e., being fully aware of His presence, in conversation with Him, experiencing Him in a fresh way, etc.)."

To help you wrap your brain around this phenomenon, we put "daily intimacy with Christ" and having a "heart for the lost" on the same graph (see next page).

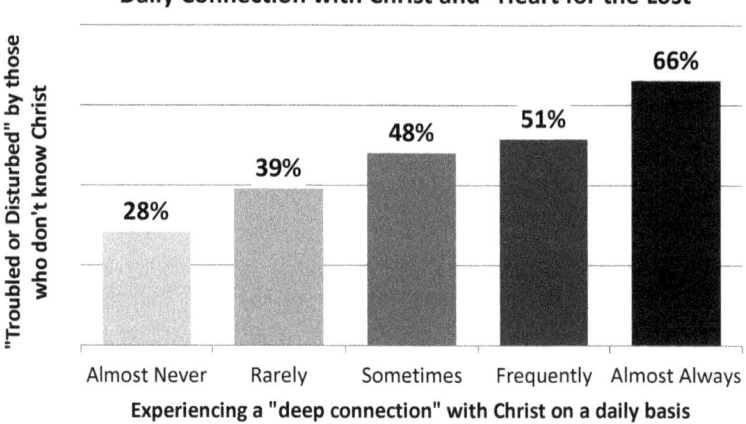

I don't know about you, but I find that graph fascinating. Let's consider a few practical implications.

What if you don't have a "heart for the lost?" Don't beat yourself up. Connect deeply with Jesus, day-in and day-out, and your attitude will begin to reflect what's on His heart. That includes being "disturbed" by the thought of those without hope. For example, you'll begin see that drunk college kid or obnoxious co-worker with a new set of eyes.

Because the more time you spend with Jesus, *the more you'll think like Jesus.*

The LifeSigns data shouldn't have surprised us, especially since scripture makes it clear, "Have this attitude in yourselves which was also in Christ Jesus." What kind of attitude is that? "In humility value others above yourselves, not looking to your own interests but each of you to the interests of the others" (Philippians 2:3-5).

And the "interests of others" encompasses much more than sharing the good news. It covers the full spectrum of physical, spiritual, and emotional needs among God's children. That's why, as you're compelled by Christ to pursue a Life with Purpose, your abilities will also be transformed.

Compelled by Grace – New Abilities

The Bible is not merely a divinely inspired self-help book, though it is helpful. It's not just a collection of sanctified success principles, though it can make you more successful. The Bible is so much more.

With the Great Commission to "go and make disciples" still ringing in their ears, the New Testament authors like Paul, Peter, James, and John wrote to people who were investing their lives in serving, leading, and building the church. Whole books like Acts, Timothy, and Thessalonians were written to guide and equip ordinary people who were, quite literally, following Christ to the ends of the earth. They had found a Life with Purpose.

Yes, scripture can teach you how to be happy and healthy, but that's far too limited. *It misses God's grand, sweeping mission to redeem all of humanity.* In my experience, the Bible takes on a whole new perspective when you're actively engaged in the wild adventure of ministering to broken people. Why? Because as you develop a Life with Purpose, you will face many of the same issues that believers faced 2,000 years ago. When your faith is stretched, whole sections of scripture will come alive for the very first time; they'll become fresh and relevant like never before.

We sometimes say to expecting mothers, "You're eating for two, so eat well." The same is true for you. As the love of Christ

CONVERSATION THREE – LIFE WITH PURPOSE

compels you to engage with messy, broken people in your everyday orbit, you'll find that you're "eating for two" every time you open your Bible. That's one of the most important ways Christ develops new abilities in you. When you get in over your head; when you come face-to-face with deep spiritual poverty, you'll scour the scriptures in search of practical answers.

"Okay, so I need to read my Bible more," you say. "Big deal." No, this isn't about cramming your skull full of theology. It's about a vibrant relationship *with Christ* and *with others*, fueled by the high-protein, non-fat truth found in the living word of God. Want proof?

Our LifeSigns data shows the number one difference among people who "frequently" or "consistently" share their faith is they frequently, "Talk with friends about what they're learning from God's Word (i.e., by sharing personal insights, asking tough questions, finding practical applications from the Bible, etc.)."

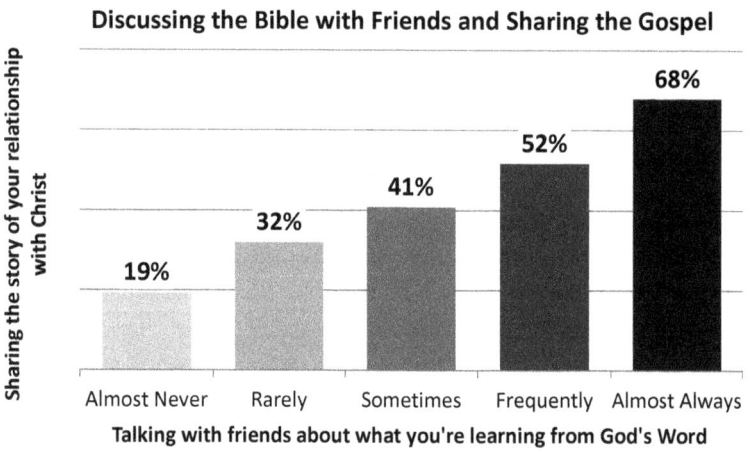

Discussing the Bible with Friends and Sharing the Gospel

As a researcher, I can tell you the graph above illustrates a powerful, statistically significant linear correlation. In plain English, when you see that perfect stair-step on the graph, it means that *these two things almost always go together*. What's more, these two items were placed at completely different sections of the

LifeSigns: How are you? Really.

LifeSigns assessment. In my opinion, our little LifeSigns experiment has uncovered one of the Holy Spirit's methods of spreading the good news of Christ: soaking in the Word.

It happened with Peter and John too. Within a few short weeks of Pentecost, more than 5,000 people had "heard the message and believed." So, the Jewish authorities arrested Peter and John and threw them in jail overnight. The next day, they were put on trial. The danger was real. The last time they put someone on trial for sharing the gospel (Jesus), they sentenced him to death on a cross. But when these religious experts "saw the courage of Peter and John and realized that they were unschooled, ordinary men, they were astonished, and they took note that these men had been with Jesus" (Acts 4:1-13).

I absolutely love that! *Unschooled, ordinary men.* More precisely, two former fishermen "astonished" the high priest and his erudite entourage by speaking with courage and conviction about the mysteries of God. How did they do it? Where did all this newfound ability come from? For one thing, they had talked with—and about—the Living Word (Jesus) for three years. Their boldness wasn't a momentary fluke, it was the product of hours and hours in conversation with Jesus.

What's more, when the religious "experts" commanded them never to speak again in the name of Jesus, Peter and John replied, "Which is right in God's eyes: to listen to you, or to Him? You be the judges! As for us, we cannot help speaking about what we have seen and heard" (Acts 4:20).

You see, they couldn't help it either.

All the stats and, more importantly, the scriptures make it clear. Talking with friends (who are safe) about what you're learning from God's Word enables you to talk with non-Christians (which is scary) about the wonders of the gospel. The two are intertwined as Christ lives through you.

We also found the number one growth priority in this section was, "to become more confident in sharing Christ." Here's the good news: You don't need to be an expert in apologetics or debate

Conversation Three – Life with Purpose

to share your story of your relationship with Christ. Do you know Jesus? Then you could do it today. That first Bible study I led by the pool, when John 3:16 was the only verse I knew, proves that God works mightily in spite of our limited knowledge and abilities. I just shared my story and pointed to scripture.

Nevertheless, Paul tells young Timothy to "do your best to present yourself to God as one approved, a worker who does not need to be ashamed and who correctly handles the word of truth." (2 Timothy 2:15). Bottom Line: *God isn't looking for scholars, but surrendered servants.*

As you allow Christ to express His life through you and pursue a Life with Purpose, you'll have real-time opportunities to develop your knowledge and skills. That applies to more than evangelism. It's true for a whole world of Christ-enabled ministry: teaching kids, counseling addicts, leading a small group, and yes, introducing someone to this incredible guy named Jesus.

Compelled by Grace – New Actions

Your behavior doesn't spontaneously spring forth without a source. Your actions, the things you say and do, reflect your heart. Proverbs 4:23 says, "Above all else, guard your heart, for *everything you do* flows from it." That's why we began with the "roots" of your behavior, including your awareness (heart) and your attitude (mind).

Now the rubber meets the road. How does the love of Christ compel you to act differently?

Two thousand years before Oprah popularized the idea of "Random Acts of Kindness," Jesus was curing leprosy, healing the lame, and washing smelly feet. But today, some pastors worry that a culture of consumerism has infiltrated the church. They know that some people "consume" Sunday services exactly as they would a movie or a ball game, and then move on to what's next in their busy schedule.

Unfortunately, the most recent LifeSigns data backs this up. Only one in three people serve weekly *after they've attended church for 6-10 years*. Less than one in ten people serve weekly in their first year at church. The old 80/20 rule of thumb says that eighty percent of ministry is done by twenty percent of the people. In reality, it may be closer to 90/10. The stats on financial giving are even more sobering, but I won't share them here. So, what's to be done?

My college pastor put it simply, "How do you know if you're called to serve? The basic answer is...when you see a need." Although you probably can't end world hunger or cure cancer, this approach is a good place to start a Life with Purpose. As your eyes are opened, you'll be compelled by Christ to "no longer live for yourself." You'll discover that every day provides a dozen opportunities to take action, both inside and outside the church.

Our LifeSigns data showed the biggest difference among people who frequently or consistently respond with action to the Holy Spirit's nudge is this: They've "allowed God to shift their focus from themselves to become more others oriented." That's one reason Christ starts with your heart.

My long-time worship pastor, Scott Dyer, often reminds us, "All of life can be an act of worship." He's right. In Romans it says, "I urge you, in view of God's mercy, to offer your bodies as a living sacrifice, holy and pleasing to God—this is your true and proper worship" (Romans 12:1).

I used to wonder, "So I'm supposed to offer my *body* as a *living sacrifice*? What's up with that?"

Since God has already provided His son as the ultimate sacrifice for sin, today our "living sacrifices" are purely an act of worship. This verse explodes the boundaries of worship beyond what happens on Sunday morning. It means you can worship God with your time and energy, with your intellect and creativity, with everything you are and everything you do. When you discover the true meaning of worship, becoming more "others oriented" is natural and easy.

I've noticed that as people mature in Christ, and as they worship Him with their whole life, an important change takes place. They begin to "take off the bib and put on the apron." They move from being fed to doing the feeding. They've made the transition from being served to doing the serving. And underneath it all, *they're really just worshiping God.*

What's more, this kind of Christ-compelled action is one of the most reliable indicators that you're maturing in Christ. It's the unmistakable fruit of a life planted and watered by the hand of the master gardener (John 15). It's the hallmark of a life with Purpose.

So, here's the big question: *Are you seeing a change from being self-focused to become more others-focused?* If you are, it's a powerful sign that Christ is living in you and working through you. Keep going!

Compelled by Grace – New Outcomes

At the end of Jesus' explanation of the vine and branches in John 15, He reminds us that, "You did not choose me, but I chose you and appointed you so that you might go and bear fruit—fruit that will last" (John 15:16). Notice that you've been chosen for a purpose: to bear fruit that lasts forever. That means that your choices, those daily decisions you make in the ebb and flow of ordinary life, will echo for all eternity.

If you've seen the stunning film, *The Bema*, a story about meeting Jesus face-to-face in heaven, you know that some of your life's work is temporal (it won't last) and some is eternal (it lasts forever). As you review your LifeSigns results from this section, try asking yourself what they call the Bema question: *Am I living for "The Day," or just today?*

LifeSigns: How are you? Really.

Life with Purpose: Roots and Fruits

Paul said it best, "Christ will make his home in your hearts as you trust in him. Your roots will grow down into God's love and keep you strong" (Ephesians 3:17). When Christ takes up residence in your heart and His grace compels you; when you get so close to Jesus that you see the world with His eyes; when you listen for and follow His leading—then you will see new growth from the "roots" all the way to the "fruits" in your life.

You won't be able to help it.

What does it mean to live for "The Day?"
Watch a 3-minute intro to *The BEMA* film:
vimeo.com/28768611

You can order The BEMA movie at theBema.org.

Conversation Three – Life with Purpose

LifeSign #1: Becoming Others-Oriented

Surrender: Allowing God to SHIFT your focus to be more OTHERS oriented (as you go through each day, listening and looking for opportunities to be used by God)

Conversation Starters

What do you think?
1. What percent of the time do we spend primarily thinking about ourselves?
2. How can you make the shift from focusing primarily on yourself to genuinely becoming "others-oriented?"

What does God say?

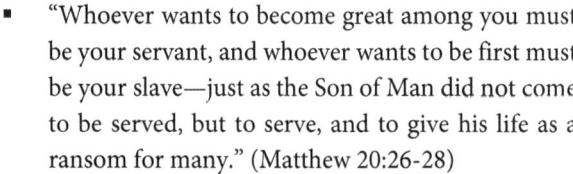
Biblical Foundations

- "Whoever wants to become great among you must be your servant, and whoever wants to be first must be your slave—just as the Son of Man did not come to be served, but to serve, and to give his life as a ransom for many." (Matthew 20:26-28)
- "Do not merely look out for your own personal interests, but also for the interests of others." (Philippians 2:4)

Okay, so now what?

Ideas for Growth

- Try serving in secret. Identify one practical way you can serve someone today—especially something that nobody will see, and you won't get the credit. Now go do it!
- Read *The Heart of a Servant: Letters from Jack Miller* by C. John Miller. These letters by a seasoned, influential pastor address a variety of ministry issues, as well as physical suffering, overcoming sin, learning to forgive, spiritual warfare, etc.

Your Next Step: _____
_____
_____

LifeSigns: How are you? Really.

LifeSign #2: Caring for "the Least of These"

Compassion in Action: You know God cares deeply for "the least of these." Stretching yourself to meet the NEEDS of people outside your comfort zone (the elderly, addicted, sick, unemployed, or in prison)

Conversation Starters

What do you think?
1. Define your comfort zone. Where does it start and where does it stop?
2. Share one real-life opportunity where you can love someone outside your comfort zone.
3. What is holding you back? Be honest.

What does God say?

Biblical Foundations

- "Religion that God our Father accepts as pure and faultless is this: To look after orphans and widows in their distress and to keep oneself from being polluted by the world." (James 1:2) See James 1.
- "As God's chosen people, holy and dearly loved, clothe yourselves with compassion, kindness, humility, gentleness and patience." (Colossians 3:12)

Okay, so now what?

Ideas for Growth

- Need perspective on compassion? Check out *Jesus in the Margins* by Rick McKinley, or *The Purpose Driven Life* by Rick Warren. Both available at ChristianBook.com (a good alternative to Amazon).
- Consider adopting a child in an undeveloped country. You'll exchange letters and pictures, pray for each other, and get a glimpse into how a small investment can make a big impact. Check out Compassion International (Compassion.com) or World Vision (WorldVision.org).

Your Next Step: _____
_____
_____

Conversation Three – Life with Purpose

LifeSign #3: Serving with Your Gifts

Serving Others: Using your GIFTS and PASSIONS to serve others (loving your neighbors across the street or across the globe, inside the church or out in your world)

Conversation Starters

What do you think?
1. Quick. What are your top three gifts? Don't worry about the terminology, just talk about what comes effortlessly.
2. Share one example of how you've allowed God to use your gifts to bless others. It doesn't have to be church-related. Anything goes.

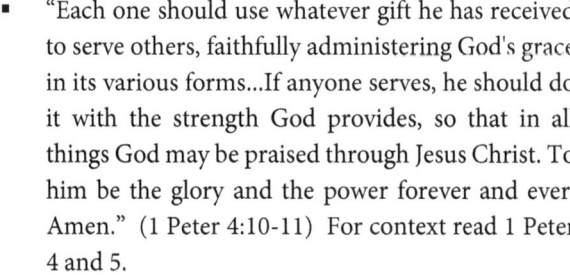
Biblical Foundations

What does God say?
- "Each one should use whatever gift he has received to serve others, faithfully administering God's grace in its various forms...If anyone serves, he should do it with the strength God provides, so that in all things God may be praised through Jesus Christ. To him be the glory and the power forever and ever. Amen." (1 Peter 4:10-11) For context read 1 Peter 4 and 5.
- "Since you are eager to have spiritual gifts, try to excel in gifts that build up the church." (1 Corinthians 14:12

Ideas for Growth

Okay, so now what?
- Don't know what gifts you have? Go to www.spiritualgiftstest.com for free gifts tests for both adults and youth.
- Don't know your passions? Make a list of things that really "bother you" when you look at the world today. Pick up a copy of *Who Is My Neighbor* by Steve Moore.

Your Next Step: _____
_____
_____

LifeSigns: How are you? Really.

LifeSign #4: Developing a Heart for the Lost

The Lost: Jesus said He'd leave the 99 in order to find the one lost sheep. Are you disturbed or bothered when you think about someone who does not know Jesus personally? (seeing people in light of eternity, as alive or dead, just as God sees them)

Conversation Starters

What do you think?
1. Why is it hard to see people from an eternal perspective?
2. How do you get "eternal eyeballs?"
3. Who do you know personally, that doesn't have a relationship Christ? Does that "bother you?"

Biblical Foundations

What does God say?
- "Just as man is destined to die once, and after that to face judgment, so Christ was sacrificed once to take away the sins of many people." (Hebrews 9:27)
- "Then Jesus came to them and said, 'All authority in heaven and on earth has been given to me. Therefore, go and make disciples of all nations, baptizing them in the name of the Father and of the Son and of the Holy Spirit, and teaching them to obey everything I have commanded you. (Matthew 28:18-20)

Ideas for Growth

Okay, so now what?
- Go on a "prayer walk" in your neighborhood. Look at each house and ask God for opportunities to engage in a relationship with your neighbors.
- Make a list of people whom you may not know Christ. Then pray for God to open their hearts to spiritual conversations, and second, for grace and strength for yourself to obey the Spirit's prompting when He reveals opportunities.

Your Next Step: _____
_____
_____

Conversation Three – Life with Purpose

LifeSign #5: Listening to People's Story

Discovery: Given the opportunity, ASKING people who may not know Jesus to share their STORY (listening out of genuine interest, to build a relationship, to pray for them)

Conversation Starters

What do you think?
1. Why ask people, especially those who don't know Christ, to share their story with you?
2. When people take a risk and share their story, what is happening beneath the surface?

Biblical Foundations

What does God say?
- "My dear brothers, take note of this: Everyone should be quick to listen, slow to speak, and slow to become angry." (James 1:19)
- "A fool finds no pleasure in understanding but delights in airing his own opinions." (Proverbs 18:2)
- "He who answers before listening—that is his folly and his shame." (Proverbs 18:13)

Ideas for Growth

Okay, so now what?
- Listening requires love. Everyone has a story and longs to be loved, but few people are willing to actually listen to them. Gently ask someone who may not know Christ or go to church to share their story with you...and listen with your whole heart.
- Listening builds trust. When you lovingly, patiently, and genuinely listen to someone's story, they've let you into their heart. Eventually, you'll earn the opportunity to share some of your story with them, including how you first met Jesus. Your salvation story is an easy, non-threatening way to share the gospel.

Your Next Step: _____
_____
_____

LifeSigns: How are you? Really.

LifeSign #6: Sharing your Story

Reaching Out: When God prompts you, being willing to share YOUR story of your relationship with Christ (how you first met, how you gave your life to Him, and how your life is different today)

Conversation Starters

What do you think?
1. Take turns sharing your three-minute life story:
   Part 1 – What were you like before Christ?
   Part 2 – How did you meet Jesus?
   Part 3 – What's different now?

Biblical Foundations

What does God say?
- "Because we loved you so much, we were delighted to share with you not only the gospel of God but our lives as well." (1 Thessalonians 2:8)
- "But in your hearts set apart Christ as Lord. Always be prepared to give an answer to everyone who asks you to give the reason for the hope that you have. But do this with gentleness and respect." (1 Peter 3:15)

Ideas for Growth

Okay, so now what?
- Engage with everyday people you normally encounter: people at work, at the kids' games, at the dry cleaner, the gas station attendant, the school crossing guard, the grocery store clerk, etc. They all have names, families, joys and struggles. They all long to be loved. They all need Jesus.
- Learn the names of your neighbors. Find creative ways to invite people who live around you into your home. Pray for opportunities to serve them (i.e., getting their mail when out of town). Be open and ready to share your story, even as you're learning about their story. It's easy, natural, and fun.

Your Next Step: _____
_____
_____

Conversation Three – Life with Purpose

LifeSign #7: Confidence in Sharing Christ

Confidence: Becoming CONFIDENT in answering questions about the Gospel of Christ ("Is Jesus the only way?" "How do we know the Bible is true?" "What about people who've never heard?")

CONVERSATION STARTERS

What do you think?
1. What are some difficult questions about the gospel have you heard over the years? Or asked yourself?
2. What's more important: Winning the argument, or loving the arguer? (Hint: 1 Corinthians 13:1-2)
3. How many questions do you have to have to answer before a skeptic will trust Jesus?

BIBLICAL FOUNDATIONS

What does God say?
- "I did not come with eloquence or superior wisdom as I proclaimed to you the testimony about God...I came to you in weakness and fear, and with much trembling. My message and my preaching were not with wise and persuasive words, but with a demonstration of the Spirit's power, so that your faith might not rest on men's wisdom, but on God's power." (1 Corinthians 2:1-5)

IDEAS FOR GROWTH

Okay, so now what?
- Head over to TheSearchforMeaning.org to hear honest conversations between two friends. They explore the most difficult questions we all have, but are afraid to ask because we might be lectured to or judged. You can download the dialogues and listen in your car or in your small group.
- Let Josh McDowell answer the tough questions for you. Buy a few copies of his little book, *More than a Carpenter*, and slide one across the table as you meet with your friend at Starbucks.

YOUR NEXT STEP: _____
_____
_____

Conversation Four

Your Work Life

"Whatever you do, work at it with all your heart, as working for the Lord, not for human masters."
– Colossians 3:23

How many of these conflicting messages about the nature of work have you heard over the years?

- Is work a curse? Or is work a blessing?
- Is work secular? Or is work spiritual?
- Is work your priority? Or is family your priority?
- Is work temporal? Or is work of eternal value?
- Do you work for a paycheck? Or to make a difference?

With so many mixed messages, no wonder it's hard to figure out how your Christian faith relates to your work life. It's easy to get cynical about the whole thing. But if you really believe work is simply about getting a paycheck, that means you're investing two-thirds of your life on nothing more than a "necessary evil."

That makes zero sense.

Perhaps that's why the number one growth priority in the Work Life section of LifeSigns isn't learning how to deal with work-related stress. It's not about finding a job that's a good fit for your gifts and abilities. It isn't even about balancing your time between work and family. By a wide margin, the top priority was, "Working to honor God, rather than just to impress others or get ahead (i.e., serving Christ, regardless of the kind of work you do)." Thousands of people, just like you, crave a Christ-centered purpose in their work life.

Most of us have not found it.

In their excellent book, *Your Work Matters to God*, the authors begin with an intriguing premise: "Every day, millions of people go to work without seeing the slightest connection between what they do all day and what they think God wants done in the world. For example, you may sell insurance, yet you may have no idea whether God wants insurance to be sold. Does selling insurance matter to God or not? If not, you're wasting your life."

Whether you flip burgers or flip houses for a living, your work represents an opportunity to honor God, to put your faith into action, and to impact the world along the way.

The Real Issue: Who do you work for?

I worked for a global consulting firm for twelve years before launching and running my own business for the last ten years. Whether I was working as an employee or as the boss, I've always wrestled with an uncomfortable duplicity — there's my work life and there's my spiritual life. To use a metaphor, those two machines don't always run on the same operating system.

Don't get me wrong. Both work and ministry get my best efforts. Both career and Christ matter deeply to me. But I've always kind of followed two sets of rules, depending on the venue. There are two different ways of getting things done. And if I'm honest, there are often two different sets of motives.

SITUATIONAL CHRISTIANITY

I remember the first time I was asked to *lie to a client*.

This wasn't life or death. We were late with a big deliverable and if I would just bend the facts a little, we could smooth over a sticky situation. I like getting a paycheck, but eventually, I plucked up the courage to tell the senior consultant, "I'm sorry, but I just can't lie to the client." You know what happened next? *He lied for me.* You see, he was being "smart and strategic," whereas I was just being "idealistic." Even today in my own company, I'm offered an enticing stream of opportunities to shape the truth. It happens on almost every project.

Ken Blanchard popularized the concept of Situational Leadership years ago. Well, sometimes I feel like a situational Christian, especially at work. The worst part? I've grown accustomed to the dissonance. In other words, I've been doing it for so long, it almost feels normal.

You've probably heard the passage where Jesus taught, "No one can serve two masters. Either you will hate the one and love the other, or you will be devoted to the one and despise the other. You cannot serve both God and money" (Matthew 6:24). Obviously, the context of this passage is how we handle money. But Jesus is raising a larger issue. It's something pastors call "Lordship." Namely, who and what are you living for? Who is the CEO of your life?

It matters because who you serve determines how you serve.

When something, or someone, other than Christ is in the driver's seat, you're forced to compartmentalize. Over time, you tend to develop different ways of operating, depending on whether you're at work, with family and friends, or at church.

Here's how compartmentalizing can look (see below):

THE DIVIDED LIFE – "MANY MASTERS"

| WORK | MONEY | FAMILY | FRIENDS | CHURCH |

But how does it feel to compartmentalize? Depending on the situation, it can make you feel like a fraud. When I'm serving different masters, I've found there's a vague sense of guilt hanging in the air, a niggling reminder that all is not right. As James puts it in his discussion on living by faith in times of testing, "Their loyalty is divided between God and the world, and they are unstable in everything they do." (James 1:8).

This same frustration pops up in the LifeSigns data on work life. The vast majority of people say their top priority is to find a way to "honor God in my work." But how do you bridge the gulf between your work life and your Christian life?

A BETTER WAY: WORKING FOR THE LORD

In my little company, The Project Board in Scott's office is mission control. Oh sure, we've tried a number of fancy software platforms, but nothing works like a big whiteboard to lay it all out. It shows every client project, including the timeline, scope, and deliverables. The project board is where priorities are juggled, and decisions get made. It's also where we discover that we've inadvertently promised to deliver three huge projects—all in the same week.

My staff has developed a love/hate relationship with this thing. It can be a relentless and unforgiving taskmaster, but it also keeps us from killing each other.

LifeSigns: How are you? Really.

Right in the middle of our project board, I've taped a sign that looks just like this:

> **Remember, every day...**
>
> "Whatever you do, whether in word or deed, do it all in the name of the Lord Jesus, giving thanks to God the Father through him."
>
> "Whatever you do, work at it with all your heart, as working for the Lord, not for human masters, since you know that you will receive an inheritance from the Lord as a reward. It is the Lord Christ you are serving."
> (Colossians 3:17, 23-24)

This little sign is helpful in several ways. First, it's a crystal-clear reminder of who's the boss—and it's not me. It reminds us that every day, we're "working for the Lord, not for human masters." That's how work becomes worship, which sounds very spiritual, but can be difficult to put into practice. So, let me translate. Our simple goal is to honor God by serving every client, even the grumpy, demanding, and unreasonable ones, "in the name of the Lord Jesus," rather than in the name of profit alone. It's real and it works.

Second, and perhaps more practically, the big truth on that little sign has become a daily prayer. Everybody is doing more with less these days. No matter what role you play at work, it's easy to get overwhelmed and cut corners. Notice the scripture says to do your work "with all your heart." God wants your absolute best efforts, so why not ask for His help?

And don't miss another nugget buried in that verse, especially when you're feeling under-valued at work. We're told to "give thanks to God the Father" in the middle of it all. Genuine gratitude is a powerful antidote to all manner of workplace frustrations, especially when you're doing all the work and getting none of the credit.

Finally, the concept of "Lordship" applies to more than the rough and tumble world of work. According the verse on our little sign, Jesus is Lord in "whatever you do, in word or deed." Rather than a selective application of your Christianity, dependent on the situation, the idea is simple: follow one leader and one Lord in every area of your life. Not once in a while, but as a daily decision to listen for His voice and follow His lead. Here's how that can look (see below):

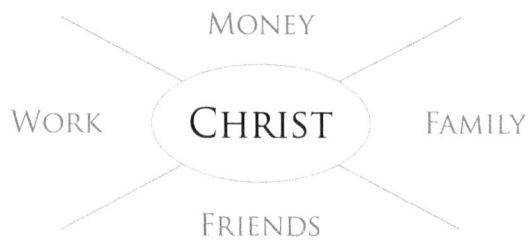

THE INTEGRATED LIFE – "ONE MASTER"

MONEY

WORK   CHRIST   FAMILY

FRIENDS

Putting Christ at the center makes for more than a clever graphic. It's like upgrading to a totally new operating system. In corporate parlance, living an integrated life under Christ requires a radical "re-org," one that completely changes your "reporting structure."

MEET THE NEW BOSS

Let's get practical, because this idea of Lordship is difficult to apply in the unforgiving arena of work—an environment that can feel a million miles away from church on Sunday. When you report to the Lord Christ, you're accountable to Him for your efforts. As with any new boss, it's imperative to understand His expectations for your role. Have you ever prayed, "Lord, what do you want done today? And *how* do you want me to do it?"

Is that too simplistic? It wasn't for the apostle Paul.

One of the first verses I memorized as I left grad school for the wild frontier of corporate life was this: "Am I now trying to win the approval of men, or of God? Or am I trying to please men? If

I were still trying to please men, I would not be a servant of Christ" (Galatians 1:10).

Notice that, in the past, Paul was trying to please people. Then his allegiance changed. His radical re-org put him under new management. Paul's courage and candor in the most difficult situations, his methods and message, were all transformed once he sought the approval of God, not people.

As of today, I want to challenge you to start reporting to a new boss: The Lord Jesus Christ.

As you devote yourself to Christ at work, your motives will begin to flow from a new source. Christ will increase your risk tolerance because your faith is in Him, not just in your own abilities. In my experience, working in Christ's power changes how you handle everything from cut-throat office politics to angry customers, from contract negotiations to something as mundane as the use of sick days. The bottom line: Working for Jesus is freeing and fulfilling like nothing else.

As you review your LifeSigns results from the Work Life section, ask yourself, "How would my view of struggles at work change if I knew I was *under new management?*"

Conversation Four – Work Life

LifeSign #1: Dealing with Work Stress

Dealing with Stress: Handling the PRESSURE at work in a healthy way (trusting Christ when you're frustrated or anxious, relying on God's grace and guidance)

Conversation Starters

What do you think?
1. What's your biggest source of stress at work these days? Be specific.
2. How can your reliance on Christ reduce your stress level at work?

Biblical Foundations

What does God say?
- "Jesus said, "Come to me, all of you who are weary and carry heavy burdens, and I will give you rest." (Matthew 11:28)
- "Cast your cares on the Lord and he will sustain you; he will never let the righteous fall." (Psalm 55:22)
- "Commit to the Lord whatever you do, and your plans will succeed." (Proverbs 16:3) For context read all of Proverbs 16.

Ideas for Growth

Okay, so now what?
- The effect of prayer on stress reduction has been documented in numerous studies. How is your prayer life? Consider reading *Too Busy Not to Pray* by Bill Hybels. Check out these verses: Matthew 11:28-30; John 14:27; Psalm 4:8.
- The Bible treats the body as an important concern. In 1 Thessalonians 5:13, Paul tells the church that he is praying for them "body, soul, and spirit." Stress has negative effects upon you that can be reduced through exercise and diet.

Your Next Step: _____
_____
_____

LifeSigns: How are you? Really.

LifeSign #2: Balancing Work and Life

Your Time: Effectively BALANCING your work demands with the rest of your life—saying "no" when necessary (juggling travel, family life, time with spouse/kids, project deadlines)

Conversation Starters

What do you think?
1. Is there really such a thing as "work/life balance?"
2. When have you said "no" to something at work in order to say "yes" to something at home? What happened?

Biblical Foundations

What does God say?
- "Teach us to number our days, that we may gain a heart of wisdom." (Psalm 90:12) For context read all of Psalm 90.
- "In vain you rise early and stay up late, toiling for food to eat — for He grants sleep to those He loves." (Psalm 127:2)

Ideas for Growth

Okay, so now what?
- If you don't do anything else, check out the little book *Choosing to Cheat*, by Andy Stanley. It's like a huge "permission slip" to re-prioritize your work and home life.
- Read "In Search of Work-Life Balance" by Russell Clayton. It's a biblically based, practical, and achievable way forward for anyone who's wrestling to find a functional balance between the necessity of work and the desire to spend time with those who matter the most.

Your Next Step: _____
_____
_____

Conversation Four – Work Life

LifeSign #3: Using your Gifts at Work

Job Fit: Finding a GOOD FIT at work for the gifts and abilities God has given you (it's matched to your strengths, more than just a paycheck, fulfilling and rewarding)

Conversation Starters

What do you think?
1. What are your strengths? The terminology isn't important, just share what you're really good at.
2. Now, what percent of those do you get use at work during a typical week? 30% 50%? 80%?
3. What gifts and strengths do you have that are *not* getting used at work?

Biblical Foundations

What does God say?
- "So, in Christ we, though many, form one body, and each member belongs to all the others. We have different gifts, according to the grace given to each of us." (Romans 12:5-6)
- "There are different kinds of gifts, but the same Spirit distributes them. There are different kinds of service, but the same Lord. There are different kinds of working, but in all of them and in everyone it is the same God at work." (1 Corinthians 12:4-6)

Ideas for Growth

Okay, so now what?
- Have you considered taking a self-discovery assessment? Check out StrengthsFinder.com. The Strengths Finder 2.0 assessment also has a book that is helpful in this process.
- Check out the book *48 Days to the Work You Love* by Dan Miller.

Your Next Step: _____
_____
_____

LifeSigns: How are you? Really.

LifeSign #4: Developing a Servant's Heart

Servant Attitude: Being truly motivated at work to SERVE, and even help others succeed (even when serving others takes extra effort, provides you with less credit, is outside your job description)

Conversation Starters

What do you think?
1. Who is the most difficult person at work? If you were to selflessly go out of your way to serve them, how would they react?
2. How do you "get ahead" at work? Really.

Biblical Foundations

What does God say?
- "He must become greater; I must become less." (John the Baptist, when asked about his career aspirations in John 3:30)
- "But they kept quiet because on the way they had argued about who was the greatest. Sitting down, Jesus called the Twelve and said, 'Anyone who wants to be first must be the very last, and the servant of all.'" (Jesus in Mark 9:34-35)
- "Be devoted to one another in brotherly love... Never be lacking in zeal, but keep your spiritual fervor, serving the Lord." (Romans 12:10-11)

Ideas for Growth

Okay, so now what?
- The title says it all: *The Selfless Way of Christ: Downward Mobility and the Spiritual Life*, by Henri Nouwen.
- Check out the classic little book, *The One Minute Manager* by Ken Blanchard and Spencer Johnson. The simple principles are focused on others and maps out how to love one another in the workplace.

Your Next Step: _____
_____
_____

Conversation Four – Work Life

LifeSign #5: Building Relationships at Work

New Relationships: Making CONNECTIONS with people at work who don't know Jesus or go to church (offering to grab lunch, learn about their family, interests, beliefs)

Conversation Starters

What do you think?
1. What's your definition of "the holy huddle?" What kinds of friendships do you have outside of the church?
2. Who would you like to get to know at work, that may or may not know Christ, just to build a relationship?

Biblical Foundations

What does God say?
- "Let your light shine before others, that they may see your good deeds and glorify your Father in heaven." (Matthew 5:16)
- "Though I am free and belong to no one, I have made myself a slave to everyone, to win as many as possible. To the Jews I became like a Jew, to win the Jews…To the weak I became weak, to win the weak. I have become all things to all people so that by all possible means I might save some." (Paul sharing his heart in 1 Corinthians 9:19-22)

Ideas for Growth

Okay, so now what?
- Nobody wants to feel like a "project," but everyone wants to be genuinely loved. What if you invited a co-worker and family to your house for dinner?
- Organize a group around common interests such as tennis, golf, etc. then follow up with individual members of the group. Your kindness and genuine love will make an impact.

Your Next Step: _____
_____
_____

LifeSigns: How are you? Really.

LifeSign #6: Working with Integrity

Integrity: When there's pressure to compromise at work, choosing to do the right thing (speaking up, telling the truth, being faithful with company money and time)

Conversation Starters

What do you think?
1. How have you been pressured to compromise at work? Specifically.
2. How did you handle it?
3. What were the consequences?

Biblical Foundations

What does God say?
- "I also do my best to maintain always a blameless conscience both before God and before men." (Paul on trial in Acts 24:16)
- "The one whose walk is blameless, who does what is righteous, who speaks the truth from their heart; whose tongue utters no slander, who does no wrong to a neighbor, and casts no slur on others; who despises a vile person but honors those who fear the Lord; who keeps an oath even when it hurts, and does not change their mind." (Psalm 15:2-4)
- "The Lord detests lying lips, but he delights in men who are truthful." (Proverbs 12:22)

Ideas for Growth

Okay, so now what?
- Select a friend whom you trust at work and share your challenges, pray together, hold each other accountable to work with integrity.
- Read *Your Work Matters to God* by Douglas Sherman and William D. Hendricks.

Your Next Step: _____
_____
_____

Conversation Four – Work Life

LifeSign #7: Honoring God through Work

Honoring God: Do you believe you're working to honor Christ, rather than just to impress others or get ahead? (serving God, regardless of the kind of work)

Conversation Starters

What do you think?
1. What is a work-life definition of worship?
2. What's your primary motivation at work?
3. How can your everyday work be done "unto the Lord?"

Biblical Foundations

What does God say?
- "Am I now trying to win the approval of men, or of God? Or am I trying to please men? If I were still trying to please men, I would not be a servant of Christ." (Paul in Galatians 1:10)
- "Whatever you do, work at it with all your heart, as working for the Lord, not for men." (Paul in Colossians 3:23)
- "I will not venture to speak of anything except what Christ has accomplished through me…" (Romans 15:18)

Ideas for Growth

Okay, so now what?
- Make yourself a little sign with Colossians 3:23 on it. Put it somewhere that you can see every day at work. Pray that God would transform your work into an act of worship.
- Grab some buddies at work, find a quiet spot, and pray together for your day. Together, ask God to help you make a difference and touch people. See what happens next!

Your Next Step: _____
_____
_____

Conversation Five

Looking for Work

*"I sought the Lord, and he answered me;
he delivered me from all my fears."*
– Psalm 34:4

For fun, we called it the "Radical Résumé Makeover."

We'd gather friends who were out of work, in transition, or looking for their first real job out of college and put a shine on their faces and on their résumés as best we could.

Every time we do one of our Makeovers, I'm always struck by how emotionally difficult it is to be out of work. It affects so many areas of your life. See if you can relate to some of the things we've heard:

"Staying at home is depressing to me, isolating, and lonely."
"I have fear of mounting bills and debts."

Conversation Five – Looking for Work

"I'm so tired of waiting. Wondering."
"I feel worthless, like I am not making a difference in someone's life."
"I am feeling pretty defeated, but I remind myself on a daily basis that God has a position waiting for me. I'm just so tired."
"I am scared."
"I'm lonely. I'm tired of hurting. I just want the pain to stop. And I want to be around people again. I have to trust God, but sometimes it's just hard."

I've been there, my friend. It's one thing to lose your income, but several years ago as a new business owner, I got to experience the double-whammy of *negative income*. When you own the company, everybody gets paid before you do: employees, vendors, contractors, and the IRS. Over a period of months, I not only went without a paycheck, but I had to actually put money into the business to cover payroll and operating expenses. It's like you're the last person in line at the buffet, but when it's your turn, all the food is gone, and you still have to pay the bill.

Trust me, it got old very quickly.

For me, the grey skies of unemployment and reduced income cast a pall over everything. I remember the unwelcome feelings of despair that invaded my mind and heart at strange moments: while watching the kids' game, while listening to a sermon, and of course when trying to sleep. I looked longingly at people with everyday jobs, even crappy jobs. They seemed so lucky. All the joy and color drained from my life. Even food didn't taste very good. Can you relate?

Then there's the job interviews. You need to look your best when you're feeling your worst. That's why being without an income is an opportunity to trust God like never before. Listen, one way or another, this season of unemployment will pass. It will…eventually.

So, I want to encourage you, *don't miss this moment.*

LifeSigns: How are you? Really.

You may not like it, but there is tremendous value in being forced to deepen your dependence on God in real and practical ways. Apart from a serious illness, this season of your life—this purgatory you wish would end as quickly as possible—holds the potential for hidden riches.

If you and I met at Starbucks to talk about this section of your LifeSigns, I'd look you in the eye and ask you to agree to an unusual premise: Let's agree that there some are things God wants to reach deep in your heart and character, fundamental things about your faith, that He could not access if you were fully employed. As my buddy Paul Miller says, "God is always up to something. What is it?"

Since we can't meet in-person right now, promise me that you'll stay with this virtual conversation. Don't bail, and don't skip over something you might have heard before.

God is up to something important in your life.

You don't want to miss it.

Back to Square One: Who do you trust?

Your ability to trust God during this season is entirely dependent on believing what's true, rather than being overwhelmed by your negative emotions or your difficult circumstances.

Here's what's true: *God is your provider.*

Jesus devoted a lot of time to helping people in the first century, many of whom lived on the ragged edge of poverty and hunger, to grasp this fundamental truth. I know you've read this text before, but you've got to really own it, now more than ever.

In Matthew 6, Jesus begins with, "Therefore I tell you, do not worry about your life, what you will eat or drink; or about your body, what you will wear. Is not life more than food, and the body more than clothes?"

I know what you may be thinking. "Don't worry about food and clothes? I have two car payments, a maxed-out Visa card, and a mortgage that was due last week." I hear you loud and clear. But

CONVERSATION FIVE – LOOKING FOR WORK

Jesus is trying to recalibrate your compass in the middle of this storm. You feel like your ship is sinking and you're the only one on deck holding a bucket. That's not true. Listen to your Lord.

Jesus said, "Look at the birds of the air; they do not sow or reap or store away in barns, and yet your heavenly Father feeds them. Are you not much more valuable than they?"

Stop right there.

Notice that Jesus is talking about *your value*. You have profound intrinsic worth in the eyes of God, even if all 27 companies you've asked for a job don't see it yet. Hang on to that truth and don't let go, especially when you get rejection letters.

Jesus continues, "Can any one of you by worrying add a single hour to your life? And why do you worry about clothes? See how the flowers of the field grow. They do not labor or spin. Yet I tell you that not even Solomon in all of his splendor was dressed like one of these. If that is how God clothes the grass of the field, which is here today and tomorrow is thrown into the fire," now don't miss this, "will he not much more clothe you—you of little faith?"

Notice that Jesus is putting together two critical components: (1) God's provision and (2) your faith. In addressing you with the phrase "you of little faith," he's not scolding you—he's trying to encourage you. God knows your faith has taken a beating lately. He knows that hope is in short supply and that worry is a constant companion. With simple, everyday examples right outside your window, like birds and flowers, Jesus is sending an unmistakable message, "You can trust me in the middle of the storm. I've got you."

He continues, "So do not worry, saying, 'What shall we eat?' or 'What shall we drink?' or 'What shall we wear?' For the pagans run after all these things, and your heavenly Father knows that you need them." God knows the balance in your checkbook down to the penny. He's weighed every ounce of food in your pantry. He's not oblivious to your desperate situation, even if it looks and feels as if you're totally alone and He's nowhere in sight. Don't believe your eyes, believe the truth. Your heavenly Father knows what you need, and He will provide.

"But Scott, if He knows, why hasn't He provided yet?" you ask. That's a fair question. In the very next verse, Jesus provides the answer, along with some very important instructions. He says, "But seek first his kingdom and his righteousness, and all these things will be given to you as well."

Here's your job search strategy: *Seek Him first.*

Notice that God is not asking you to lather yourself into a display of emotion or offer some religious sacrifice. He wants something far more costly. God wants your heart—and everything that goes with it—even the fear and anger and doubt. He's trying to get your undivided attention. At a time when your most urgent priorities are physical and financial, Jesus is asking you to move your relationship with Him to the very top of the list.

When you do, there's promise and a payoff. The book of Hebrews says, "without faith it is impossible to please God, because anyone who comes to him must believe that he exists and that he rewards those who earnestly seek him" (Hebrews 11:6). God rewards those who seek Him by faith.

Let's put this in practical terms: *God wants you to seek Him as urgently and desperately as you're seeking employment.*

Why? Because He's teaching you to trust Him as your ultimate provider.

Time Out: Reality Check

Since it's just you and me, sitting here at the virtual Starbucks, I'm going to say something I couldn't possibly put into this book. It's going to sound incredibly unspiritual, but I want to be completely honest with you.

I hate having to trust Him.

Seriously. Having to trust God means something has gone wrong and I can't fix it. I'll try everything else first. Maybe it's my personality, maybe I'm just stubborn, but trusting God is not usually my first reaction to difficulty—it's my last resort. Trusting

Conversation Five – Looking for Work

God by faith means waiting, and I hate waiting. I want Him to deliver results, right now, please.

That's why it's so helpful to remember the biblical definition of faith found in Hebrews: "Now faith is the assurance of things hoped for, the conviction of things not seen" (Hebrews 11:1). Instant gratification doesn't require a drop of faith. But God wants us to seek Him first. Waiting for "things hoped for" and being convinced of "things you can't see yet" are the everyday nuts and bolts of trusting God.

That leads us to another important truth during an exhausting season of unemployment: Faith requires action.

The Next Step: Faith in Action

I left graduate school proudly clutching a newly minted diploma with a 4.0 GPA, only to run straight into the recession of 1994. Six months and three dozen interviews later, still no job.

Now picture this: I'm married, broke, unemployed, and we've just traveled 500 miles *to move back in with my parents.* You know that creepy feeling when you visit your old bedroom at your parents' house? It's like entering a time capsule of your misspent youth, carefully preserved right down to the posters on the walls and stuffed animals on the bed. It even smells the same.

Now imagine living there as an adult *with your wife.*

Ugh. What a painful season of waiting. I remember walking the streets of my old neighborhood, staring at the same cracks in the pavement I'd seen walking to elementary school years before, crying out to God: "I know you're real. I know you love me. *Lord you've got to come through."*

In response, God provided a verse for that endless time of painful uncertainty. I clung to it like a drowning man on a life raft. Psalm 104 says, "All creatures look to you to give them their food at the proper time. When you give it to them, they gather it up; when you open your hand, they are satisfied with good things" (Psalm 104:27-28).

Notice once again, God is the source. But notice that He provides "at the proper time," according to His timeline, not mine. What follows is the key. It says that God gives it to them and *"they gather it up."* There's a balance in God's economy between His provision and our faithful response. That's especially important as you're looking for a job. He provides. You gather it up. God is the provider—you are the gatherer.

The apostle James, who never minces words, lays it on the line in Chapter 1, "Do not merely listen to the word, and so deceive yourselves. Do what it says...whoever looks intently into the perfect law that gives freedom, and continues in it—not forgetting what they have heard, but doing it—they will be blessed in what they do" (James 1:22-24). According to James, the blessing comes when your belief in God's promises is demonstrated by your actions.

THE REST OF THE STORY

I remember the Sunday afternoon it finally happened. In disgust, I turned off the NFL game, grabbed my stuff, and drove all the way down to the Houston public library. Buried deeply on the back shelves of the third floor was a massive volume titled *Consulting Organizations Directory*. I thumbed through the pages, searching for something, anything that fit. Then consulting firm #15574 caught my eye. It was located in the big, scary metropolis of Dallas-Forth Worth, but sounded interesting. (Just now, I dug that old page from my dusty files.)

Little did I know, that needle #15574 in the haystack was a magnificent answer to all those desperate prayers for something more than a job—prayers for a place to flourish and grow.

It still wasn't easy. Firm #15574 turned me down three times over a period of five months before finding a place for me as a junior associate in the research and development group. That's a miracle in itself, given that my prior work experience consisted of being a disk jockey at a local radio station and a campus youth pastor.

Conversation Five – Looking for Work

The point is this: *God came through big time.* During the next twelve years at that firm, I was immersed in a vibrant corporate culture, exposed to powerful business principles, and given the opportunity to work with dozens of *Fortune 500* companies.

Bottom Line: With the benefit of hindsight, it turns out that God knew *exactly* what he was doing all along. And I thought he wasn't even paying attention, oh me "of little faith."

This was clearly God "opening His hand and satisfying me with good things." None of it would have happened if God hadn't convicted me to get off my butt and put some action behind my faith on a lazy Sunday afternoon.

He provided. I gathered. Both were essential.

Don't go it Alone: Faithful Friends

You're not alone. First and foremost, realize that your heavenly Father is the head of your job search and life-planning committee. So, you're meeting with Him every day, right? And you're exploring all the unique ways He's gifted you? Good.

Second, consider using your LifeSigns results as a springboard to open a dialogue with someone you trust. Tell them about your fear and how you're struggling to trust God right now. And because dreams are fragile things, talk about your hopes for the future. Don't let them wither and die. Please just be honest about how you're doing. I promise, you'll feel better.

Third, you'll find practical resources to help in your job search on the pages that follow.

Finally, remember the basic premise behind this virtual conversation: God is always up to something in your life. This season of unemployment will eventually come to an end, so don't miss this opportunity for discovery.

As you're seeking a job, learn to seek God in new and fresh ways. Look for His handiwork in your heart. Dig deeply into His Word to unearth scriptures that renew your faith in a faithful God. I'll bet they become some of your life-long favorites, reminding you of a season when you began to trust God like never before.

Go deep. Ask God the tough questions. Don't hold back. See if you can discover what's He's up to in your life.

You'll return to work a very different person.

Conversation Five – Looking for Work

LifeSign #1: Getting Support

Encouragement: Reaching out to others for SUPPORT and encouragement during your job search (connecting with others, networking, enlisting prayer partners)

Conversation Starters

What do you think?
1. Why is it worth the time/effort to build a support team around you? What's the payoff?
2. Who can you reach out to for some prayer, accountability, support, and encouragement?

Biblical Foundations

What does God say?
- "Therefore encourage one another and build each other up, just as in fact you are doing." (1 Thessalonians 5:11)
- "And the God of all grace, who called you to his eternal glory in Christ, after you have suffered a little while, will himself restore you and make you strong, firm and steadfast. To him be the power for ever and ever. Amen." (1 Peter 5:10-11) For context read I Peter 5.

Ideas for Growth

Okay, so now what?
- Consider joining a local support group, like Crossroads Career Network for job help and weekly devotionals (see CrossroadsCareer.org)
- Use this time as an opportunity to reflect on what God may have you do. Ask him to help you find the right fit in work. Consider reading a book like *48 Days to the Work You Love* by Dan Miller.

Your Next Step: _____
_____
_____

LIFESIGNS: HOW ARE YOU? REALLY.

LifeSign #2: Finding Courage in Christ

Dealing with Fear: Finding COURAGE in Christ, as you deal with fear and uncertainty (looking to Him, remembering you can do all things through Christ who gives you strength)

CONVERSATION STARTERS

What do you think?
1. What scares you most these days? Be specific; it helps.
2. Fatigue can amplify fear tenfold. How emotionally and physically depleted are you these days?

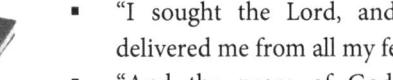

BIBLICAL FOUNDATIONS

What does God say?
- "I sought the Lord, and he answered me; he delivered me from all my fears." (Psalm 34:4)
- "And the peace of God, which transcends all understanding, will guard your hearts and your minds in Christ Jesus." (Philippians 4:7)
- "For God did not give us a spirit of timidity (fear), but a spirit of power, of love and of self-discipline." (2 Timothy 1:7) Also see 2 Timothy 1.

IDEAS FOR GROWTH

Okay, so now what?
- Read *Slaying the Giants in Your Life* by David Jeremiah, or *Psalm 91: God's Shield of Protection* by Peggy Joyce Ruth.
- On a sheet of paper make two columns. In column one, list negative ways you could respond to your situation. In column two, list ways Christ would have you respond. Pray that you would trust God to empower you to follow His leading in column two.

YOUR NEXT STEP: _____
_____
_____

CONVERSATION FIVE – LOOKING FOR WORK

LifeSign #3: Trusting God to Provide

Faith: Putting your TRUST in God to meet your financial needs during this time (remembering He is the source of all life, even when you're discouraged and trying to make ends meet)

CONVERSATION STARTERS

What do you think?
1. Where are you financially these days?
2. Do you really trust God? Do you really believe He will come through? If not, why not?
3. How might God use the pressure created by being out of work to help you make significant changes in your spending, approach to debt, or lifestyle?

BIBLICAL FOUNDATIONS

What does God say?
- "Therefore I tell you, do not worry about your life, what you will eat or drink; or about your body, what you will wear...Look at the birds of the air; they do not sow or reap or store away in barns, and yet your heavenly Father feeds them. Are you not much more valuable than they? Who of you by worrying can add a single hour to his life?" (Matthew 6:25-27) For context read Matthew 6.

IDEAS FOR GROWTH

Okay, so now what?
- Consider taking a class like Financial Peace University or Crown Financial. Seek financial counseling for help with financial decision making and budgeting.
- You can find practical tools, resources, and information to help you manage your finances from a Biblical worldview at DaveRamsey.com.

YOUR NEXT STEP: _____
_____
_____

LifeSigns: How are you? Really.

LifeSign #4: Seeking God's Direction

Seeking Direction: Carefully LISTENING for God's voice to guide your search for what's next in your career (asking Him to reveal His will, plans, and priorities for you)

CONVERSATION STARTERS

What do you think?
1. How do you "hear" God's voice best?
2. What are you hearing or sensing from God? Where is God leading you to focus your job search?
3. Do you really trust God to provide? Do you really believe He will come through? If not, why not?

BIBLICAL FOUNDATIONS

What does God say?
- "'For I know the plans I have for you,' declares the Lord, 'plans to prosper you and not to harm you, plans to give you hope and a future.'" (Jeremiah 29:11)
- "We can make our plans, but the Lord determines our steps." (Proverbs 16:9)
- "The plans of the diligent lead surely to advantage." (Proverbs 21:5)

IDEAS FOR GROWTH

Okay, so now what?
- Use this time as an opportunity to reflect on what God may have you do. Ask him to help you find the right fit in work. Consider reading a book like *48 Days to the Work You Love* by Dan Miller.
- Ask for the pastors at your church to pray with you after services on Sundays, or even over the phone.

YOUR NEXT STEP: _____
_____
_____

Conversation Six

Student Life

"Let no one look down on your youthfulness."
– 1 Timothy 4:12

I began college in the wrong major, with the wrong attitude, and with all the wrong friends.

Let's start with the friends. I didn't have the advantage of knowing Christ before heading off to college. Our wing of the dormitory was so wild, we made the school newspaper for holding keg parties (on a dry campus no less), loud music, crazy stunts (mattress surfing down the stairs), and housing a six foot Boa constrictor named *Pierre* that made un-announced appearances in the showers to terrify unsuspecting freshmen.

Okay, I'll admit this was not the best environment for the pursuit of academic excellence. I didn't care. I was having fun.

Conversation Six – Student Life

Most of that first semester was filled with late nights out and very little studying. My grades suffered as a result. But once I accepted Christ in my second semester, it was painfully clear that my buddies were pulling me in the wrong direction.

I was also a card-carrying member of the "major of the month club." Bouncing from engineering to communications to business pushed the length of my bachelor's degree to five years and accumulated a mountain of credits.

As a high school or college student, whether full or part-time, your LifeSigns will help to pinpoint any number of growth opportunities: finding a good fit for your gifts, developing healthy relationships, or perhaps simply dealing with the stress of endless homework.

Over the course of my college years, regardless of the challenges at hand, I clung to this promise: "We are God's masterpiece. He has created us anew in Christ Jesus, so we can do the good things he planned for us long ago" (Ephesians 2:10).

What "good things?" Well, I slowly realized that included in God's plan for my life, He also (1) provided me with protection and direction, (2) developed my character, and (3) instilled in me a clear sense of purpose and direction. He will for you too.

Let's touch on each of these three areas as you prepare to discuss your LifeSigns results on your life as a student.

God's Masterpiece #1: He provides you with protection and direction

At first, staying behind in an empty dorm as all my old friends hit the town on a Saturday night was difficult and lonely. I'd learned enough to realize that, "the companion of fools will suffer harm" (Proverbs 13:20). So, I sat alone in my dorm room wondering, *"Okay Lord, binge drinking and bar-hopping is not your will for my life. So now what?"*

As a parent, I'm secretly praying that my kids don't come home from college with pierced tongues, a collection of tattoos, and a taste for heavy metal music. On the other hand, I realize that my kids' heart and character are far more important than their taste in music or clothes. Honestly, my real fear is that they get mixed up with the wrong crowd.

During my season as a student, one scripture in particular offered me both protection from my old way of life and direction for the new: "Flee the evil desires of youth and pursue righteousness, faith, love and peace, along with those who call on the Lord out of a pure heart" (2 Timothy 2:22).

This verse is loaded with practical guidance. First, notice the two action-packed verbs: flee and pursue. Both are critical. It is not enough to tip toe around all the bad stuff—*run from it*. Flee! Second, notice the balance. You must also zealously *pursue* the good stuff—righteousness, faith, love, and peace. Be intentional about both fleeing and pursuing, or as I discovered, you'll get pulled back into the muck.

Finally, don't miss the last part of the verse. The key to all of this is to hang out, "with those who call on the Lord out of a pure heart." In doing so, God graciously provides both protection and direction.

Your circle of friends will have a tremendous impact on your walk with Christ and your GPA, for better or for worse. Pick the right peers and it will make all the difference in your world. As a bonus, your parents will sleep better at night.

God Masterpiece #2: He develops your character

After I hosted my first Bible study up in my dorm room, something changed. The guys on the hall looked at me in a different light, and it felt weird. I was being watched. When people at school find out you're a Christian, you too will be watched, especially by people who are curious or skeptical about Christianity.

Conversation Six – Student Life

The apostle Paul's wise advice to young Timothy became my mission statement for those turbulent years at college: "Don't let anyone look down on you because you are young, but set an example for believers in speech, in conduct, in love, in faith and in purity." (1 Timothy 4:12).

Translation: Be an example that others will want to follow.

Peer pressure and campus culture will *push* you to do things you'll regret, and they'll *pull* you away from Christ. Push back. You can be a model of maturity in a sea of stupidity—and glorify God in the process. Run through that verse again and ask yourself, "How can I be a positive example in my speech, my conduct, my faith, and in my purity?" Have the courage to go against the flow, and people will notice. You'll be a leader and not even know it.

I'd also encourage you to read the chapters in this book on "Life with Jesus" and "Life with People." All the biblical truths we discuss in those chapters will help you flourish during your tenure as a student.

God Masterpiece #3: He puts a Dream in your Heart

Whether you're in high school, smack-dab in the middle of college, or returning to school later in life—everybody expects you to figure out what you're going to be "when you grow up."

That's a ton of pressure.

Unfortunately, most of us are not like my best friend David. Dave knew exactly what he wanted to be, all the way back in fifth grade: *a rocket scientist.* No kidding. Well I'm happy to report that after getting his bachelor's, master's, and doctorate in aerospace engineering, today Dave is designing top secret space weapons for the United States Defense Department. It's all highly classified, so I really have no idea what David does, but he assures me that it's extremely cool.

Well guess what? I still don't know what I'm supposed to do when I grow up. Do you?

LifeSigns: How are you? Really.

This isn't the time or the place to advise you on how to pick a major. A quick search on Amazon will yield dozens of excellent resources. However, this is a good place to ask an important question: What does God want you to do with your life? Who is he preparing you to be when you "grow up?"

Consider how the apostle Paul answered the same question. This is important—so don't skim, you busy student. (There will be a pop quiz after.)

> *"Though I am free and belong to no one, I have made myself a slave to everyone, to win as many as possible. To the Jews I became like a Jew, to win the Jews. To those under the law I became like one under the law (though I myself am not under the law), so as to win those under the law. To those not having the law I became like one not having the law (though I am not free from God's law but am under Christ's law), so as to win those not having the law. To the weak I became weak, to win the weak. I have become all things to all people so that by all possible means I might save some. I do all this for the sake of the gospel, that I may share in its blessings"* (1 Corinthians 9: 19-23).

Pop Quiz: What was Paul's job description?

After reading that manifesto, it sounds like Paul's job description is that of a traveling evangelist. You may be surprised to know that Paul's resume included much more. Our multi-talented apostle also had extensive experience in leadership development, conflict resolution, theological study, church planting, teaching, growth strategy, pastoring, creative writing, fund-raising, prison ministry, and tent building (to pay the bills).

Yet sweeping high above all those diverse pursuits, encompassing and empowering all of Paul's efforts, was a singular mission: *"I do all this for the sake of the gospel."* God put a dream into Paul's heart that took him to the ends of the earth. Regardless

Conversation Six – Student Life

of his occupation at any given moment, Paul's passion was to help people find and follow Jesus. And his passion defined and directed everything he did along the way.

I'm not saying your focus or major doesn't matter. It does. And you enjoy tremendous freedom to pursue your passions and find a career well suited to your gifts and interests. What I am saying is that no matter what you study, whether it's medicine or medieval literature, fully embrace God's magnificent mission to redeem and renew a lost world *through you*.

Recent LifeSigns research highlights the importance of this approach to your studies. We found that the top priority selected by students was also one of the lowest scored items: "Your Purpose: Are you living for something greater than yourself? (beyond finding your dream job, but also giving yourself to Christ and to a greater cause)."

You're not like a mouse in a maze, scrambling through the labyrinth of course requirements to someday be rewarded with a degree or diploma. Much more is happening beneath the surface. How do you know that's true for you?

Study Philippians 2:13 for just a moment. It says, "For God is working in you, giving you the desire and the power to fulfill his good purpose."

Now, here's your pop quiz on the verse discussed above:

Question #1: WHO is working in your life?
 A: *God himself is at work. (that one was easy)*

Question #2: WHAT is he doing?
 A: *Giving you the desire (the will) and the power (the ability).*

Question #3: WHY is God doing it?
 A: *To fulfill his good purpose for your life.*

LifeSigns: How are you? Really.

Let's make this personal and practical for you. According to Philippians 2:13, here's what's happening beneath the surface as you plow through all your coursework: God himself is at work, developing both your passions and abilities so you can fulfill His greater purpose for your life. After all, He created you and knows all about your unique gifts and talents. What more, God knows what you're truly capable of, uniquely suited to accomplish, and destined to become in this life.

God knows what you're destined to be "when you grow up," even if you're not sure yet.

Take comfort in the knowledge that God is working in you, even as you're working for your degree or diploma. And consider this question: Where do you think God is leading you during your time in school? As you allow Christ to live in you and through you, where is he taking you?

As with Paul the apostle, I'd encourage you to let the eternal purposes of God and the urgency of the gospel permeate everything you do, or plan to do, with your time, talents, and future.

If you're willing to follow Jesus, you'll be amazed where he takes you.

Conversation Six – Student Life

LifeSign #1: Dealing with Peer Pressure

Peer Pressure: When there's pressure to follow the crowd in the wrong direction, you're DELIBERATELY choosing to follow God's leading (not worrying about what people think, doing the "right thing" even when it's not popular)

Conversation Starters

What do you think?
1. What kinds of peer pressure do you face?
2. Do the people you spend time with make it easier or harder to follow Christ? How so?
3. How are you a positive influence on people around you at school?

Biblical Foundations

What does God say?
- "He who walks with wise men will be wise, But the companion of fools will suffer harm." (Proverbs 13:20)
- "How can a young person stay on the path of purity? By living according to your word. I seek you with all my heart; do not let me stray from your commands." (Psalm 119:9-10)
- "I have more insight than all my teachers, for I meditate on your statutes. I have more understanding than the elders, for I obey your precepts. I have kept my feet from every evil path so that I might obey your word." (Psalm 119:99-101)

Ideas for Growth

Okay, so now what?
- Check out *How to Stay Christian in College* by J. Budziszewski.
- This a great resource: *Thriving at College: Make Great Friends, Keep Your Faith, and Get Ready for the Real World!* by Alex Chediak.

Your Next Step: _____
_____
_____

LifeSigns: How are you? Really.

LifeSign #2: Life with Purpose

Finding Your Purpose: Living for a cause or passion GREATER than yourself (looking beyond graduating and finding a job, you're open to God's leading, to follow Him into the unknown)

Conversation Starters

What do you think?
1. It sounds cliché, but it's a good question: "What do you want to do when you grow up?" Be specific.
2. Now, as you envision your future, where does Jesus fit into your plans? Is he just along for the ride? Or are God's purposes woven into your dreams for the future?

Biblical Foundations

What does God say?
- "For we are God's workmanship, created in Christ Jesus to do good works, which God prepared in advance for us to do." (Ephesians 2:10)
- "And we know that in all things God works for the good of those who love him, who have been called according to his purpose." (Romans 8:28) For context read all of Romans 8.

Ideas for Growth

Okay, so now what?
- This book with inspire you to dream big: *Love Does: Discover a Secretly Incredible Life in an Ordinary World* by Bob Goff.
- You can get a major dose of the "big picture" from *The Purpose Driven Life* by Rick Warren. It has become a classic and totally worth a deep dive.
- To dig deeper, consider doing a personal study on vision or goal setting. Many people have benefitted from *Experiencing God: Knowing and Doing the Will of God* by Henry Blackaby.

Your Next Step: _____
_____
_____

Conversation Six – Student Life

LifeSign #3: Reaching Out

New Relationships: Making CONNECTIONS with people at school who do NOT follow Christ or go to church (offering to grab lunch, learn about their family, interests, beliefs)

Conversation Starters

What do you think?
1. What's your definition of "the holy huddle?" What kinds of friendships do you have outside of the church?
2. Who would you like to get to know at school, that may or may not know Christ, just to build a relationship?

Biblical Foundations

What does God say?
- "Let your light shine before others, that they may see your good deeds and glorify your Father in heaven." (Matthew 5:16)
- "Though I am free and belong to no one, I have made myself a slave to everyone, to win as many as possible. To the Jews I became like a Jew, to win the Jews…To the weak I became weak, to win the weak. I have become all things to all people so that by all possible means I might save some." (Paul sharing his heart for people in 1 Corinthians 9:19-22)

Ideas for Growth

Okay, so now what?
- Nobody wants to feel like a "project," but everyone wants to be genuinely loved. What if you invited someone from school to your place for dinner?
- Organize a group around common interests such as tennis, golf, etc. then follow up with individual members of the group. Your kindness and genuine love will make an impact.

Your Next Step: _____
_____
_____

LifeSigns: How are you? Really.

LifeSign #4: Working with Integrity

Integrity: Doing your own schoolwork with total INTEGRITY (completing your assignments without plagiarizing, copying others, using Google to cut corners)

Conversation Starters

What do you think?
1. How have you been tempted to compromise your integrity at school? Specifically.
2. How did you handle it?
3. What were the consequences?

Biblical Foundations

What does God say?
- "I also do my best to maintain always a blameless conscience both before God and before men." (Paul on trial in Acts 24:16)
- "The one whose walk is blameless, who does what is righteous, who speaks the truth from their heart; whose tongue utters no slander, who does no wrong to a neighbor, and casts no slur on others; who despises a vile person but honors those who fear the Lord; who keeps an oath even when it hurts, and does not change their mind." (Psalm 15:2-4)
- "The Lord detests lying lips, but he delights in men who are truthful." (Proverbs 12:22)

Ideas for Growth

Okay, so now what?
- Pick a friend you trust at school and share your challenges, pray together, hold each other accountable to work with integrity.
- Read a Proverb a day. There are 31 chapters in Proverbs, so just read the proverb that corresponds to the calendar date. Proverbs is packed with common sense wisdom for living with integrity.

Your Next Step: _____
_____
_____

Conversation Six – Student Life

LifeSign #5: Staying Sexually Pure

Sexual Purity: How are you doing when it comes to staying sexually PURE? (honoring God in both thought and action, avoiding porn or sex outside of marriage)

CONVERSATION STARTERS

What do you think?
1. Needless to say, please make sure you're having this part of the conversation with someone of the same sex.
2. There's a lot to guard: your eyes, your thoughts, your activity on social media, and your actions. How's it going in these areas? Really.

BIBLICAL FOUNDATIONS

What does God say?
- "Flee the evil desires of youth and pursue righteousness, faith, love and peace, along with those who call on the Lord out of a pure heart." (2 Timothy 2:22)
- "No temptation has overtaken you except what is common to mankind. And God is faithful; he will not let you be tempted beyond what you can bear. But when you are tempted, he will also provide a way out so that you can endure it." (1 Corinthians 10:13)

IDEAS FOR GROWTH

Okay, so now what?
- Consider reading *Every Man's Battle* by Stephen Arterburn or *Every Woman's Battle* by Shannon Ethridge. These are great resources which deal with these issues from a biblical perspective.
- Commit passages of Scripture to memory and meditate on them—God's Truth to counteract the lies of the flesh, like Romans 6.

YOUR NEXT STEP: _____
_____
_____

Conversation Seven

Your Money and Finances

"Store your treasures in heaven...for where your treasure is, there your heart will be also."
– Jesus teaching on money

This isn't about money. It's about freedom.

What do I mean by that?

It's about freedom from worry that you're not going to make it every month. Freedom from conflict with your spouse over the budget. Freedom from guilt that you're not doing the right thing with the resources God provides. It's about freedom from fear of what lies ahead, whether it's your retirement or paying for college. And it's about freedom from overdraft notices, those collection calls, and that defeated feeling that comes with being constantly behind with your finances.

Conversation Seven – Money and Finances

It's also about finding the freedom to follow your dreams. It's about having the freedom to set healthy boundaries around how much time you spend at the office, so you can spend time with the kids before they're gone. It's about the freedom to help your daughter rent her first apartment, the freedom to sponsor a child in Tanzania with Compassion International, or the freedom to give a reliable car to a single mom. It's about having the freedom to go back to school, get a certification, or unleash your talents in a start-up business. It's about the freedom to create a different family history that lasts for generations.

Ultimately, it's about having the freedom to join God in His magnificent quest, "to bring good news to the afflicted, to bind up the brokenhearted, to proclaim liberty to captives and freedom to prisoners" (Isaiah 61:1).

And you thought we were just going to talk about getting out of debt? That's way too small.

"But wait a minute, Scott," you say, "what exactly do you mean by 'it'? What's 'it' about?"

Here's your answer: *It's about Stewardship.*

Now if you're like me, a wall of resistance pops into your mind when you hear the word "stewardship." You may even be thinking about skipping the rest of this chapter.

Don't bail on me now.

Stewardship is a fantastic concept that, unfortunately, carries a bit of negative baggage. Why? Perhaps because pastors like to talk about "stewardship" when they're trying to raise money. But stewardship is so much bigger than just giving money to a church or ministry. *Stewardship applies to your whole life.* And it holds the key to freedom from financial bondage, as well as the freedom to pursue some big dreams. Good stewardship is the gateway to go places you've never imagined with your life.

If, in your mind, preachers have hijacked the idea of stewardship just to get your money, then it's time for a new perspective. When it comes to the wonderful word *stewardship*, to quote Bono from U2, "We're stealing it back."[7]

STEWARDSHIP MISTAKES

I'm raising two little capitalists.

That wasn't my intention, of course. I offered my kids a weekly allowance and the chance to earn a little extra by helping with chores around the house. My elaborate system gave them an opportunity to handle money and to develop some personal responsibility. Plus, I'd have trash night off.

It was brilliant. Or so I thought.

Apparently, I had no idea *who* I was dealing with. Within the first week, my kids were fighting over who got to take out the trash, calculating their weekly take, and even sub-contracting chores to the other kid in exchange for a cut of the action. I found myself in complex negotiations with my son (who is going to be a lawyer someday) over his "rate" when I'd ask him to do something not clearly defined on the chore chart.

It gets worse.

God forbid, I was late with my weekly payments of their allowance. I watched in horror as my two sweet children turned into merciless bill collectors, gleefully turning the screws on dear old Dad. What's more, as soon as they had some money in their pockets, it was blown in the next trip to Target or McDonalds.

How did this happen? Where did I go wrong?

I began to realize that I'd thrown my kids into the complex world of money without a solid, biblical understanding of stewardship. A windy lecture about the perils of greed wasn't going to cut it. Not with these two. But how do you translate Biblical truths about stewardship into something meaningful and memorable to a six and an eight-year old?

A decade later, the result still hangs on a big sheet of flip-chart paper in our kitchen. It has a dozen big truths about life and

---

[7] U2, *Helter Skelter*, Rattle & Hum (Island Records, 1990).

money, with "Watson Family Values" scrawled across the top. It's faded and wrinkled, and it clashes with our décor, but we've become quite fond of it. So, it stays put.

BIBLICAL STEWARDSHIP

The term stewardship includes two hugely important concepts. First, stewardship designates *ownership*. Being a steward of something means that you do *not* own it—it rightfully belongs to someone else—not you. Second, stewardship assigns *responsibility*. When you're a steward you're a manager. Essentially, you're responsible for someone else's stuff.

So, we taught the kids Big Truth #1 this way: *God owns everything: He made it. He owns it. And He loans it to me.* For fun we said it together around the kitchen table, like we were reciting the Pledge of Allegiance—only I didn't make them stand up. We also memorized Psalm 24:1 together, "The earth is the Lord's, and everything in it, the world, and all who live in it." So far, so good? Not so fast.

One quiet evening, not long after I'd unveiled my brilliant plan, unanswered work e-mail called my name. So, I asked my son, "Hey buddy, can I have my laptop back?" Quick as lightning, he shot back, "Dad, it's NOT your laptop, it's GOD's laptop."

I had to smile. At least the biblical concept of stewardship was sinking in, even if he was haggling for another ten minutes fiddling with his fantasy football team. I said, "You're right buddy. It is God's laptop, and he's asked me to use it wisely. You've had enough computer time for one night. Hand it over."

Telling you that God owns everything is a simple concept to grasp, but it's difficult to apply. Just think for a moment, do you really act like it's not your money? Of course not. Every day, you make unilateral decisions about how to spend God's money. And if you think its no big deal to spend someone else's money, that's fabulous. Can I borrow your credit card for a little shopping spree on Amazon?

You see, we don't think or act like *stewards*, we think and act like *owners*. That's the challenge.

Big Truth #2 we taught the kids about stewardship went like this: *You can do three things with God's money: spend it, save it, and share it.* To this day, the kids can recite it perfectly, but they'll groan and roll their eyes if you try to make them do it. Together we memorized Proverbs 11:25, "A generous person will prosper; whoever refreshes others will be refreshed."

It should come as no surprise that this one backfired too.

My son would gravely remind me of my biblically-ordained duty to be generous—as he'd spied a new football at the store. And, after I admonished my daughter to be generous with a portion of her allowance, she proudly announced that she'd "shared" her allowance with a friend at school—in exchange for some ice cream.

My befuddled reply was, "Okay kiddo...that's not exactly what I had in mind." Man, this stewardship thing is not as easy as it sounds, even for kids.

THE GOOD INTENTIONS GAP

If you're struggling with money and finances, you're not alone. By far, the number one priority people pick in the Money and Finances section of LifeSigns is this: "Becoming secure in your financial situation and future (i.e., knowing that God is the ultimate provider, you're able to trust Him)." Given the amount of debt we carry, it's not surprising the desire for financial security bubbled to the top.

The second set of priorities people picked all related to stewardship struggles, including: developing personal discipline, limiting frivolous spending, separating your wants from needs, and living below your means to avoid debt. For most of us, good stewardship is an ongoing struggle.

You may remember that we also gently asked a question about giving in LifeSigns. This question focused on the gap between your intentions and your actions: "Desired Giving: How do you *feel* about your financial giving these days? (i.e., to God's work with churches, ministries, the needy, etc.)" Here's what we've found (see graph below).

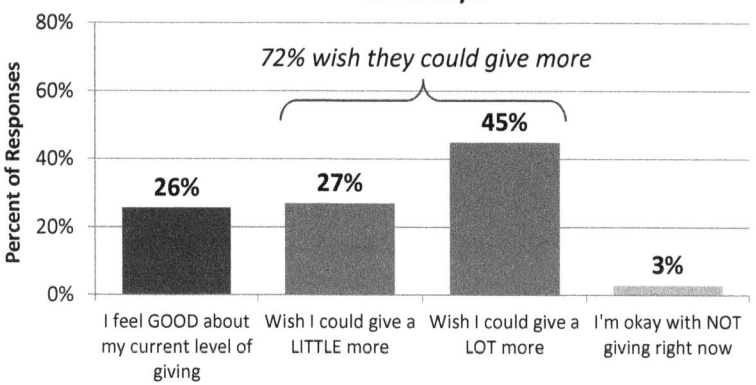

The vast majority of people, 72% to be exact, wish they could give "a little more" or "a lot more" to worthy causes. We're chock-full of good intentions. The actual stats on giving at my home church closely correlate to the LifeSigns data on giving. This next statistic comes from my church, not from LifeSigns, and has been shared publicly by the leaders. Read this carefully:

Sixty percent of the people who are regular attenders give less than $100 a year to our church.

Isn't that just awful? Who are all those selfish people? Well, to be painfully honest: *I'm one of "those people." I'm a part of the 60% who didn't give.*

Really? Why not?

This is difficult to talk about, but I'm trying to be honest with you. I used to give generously and consistently to a wide variety of ministries, not just to my home church. Annual raises and bonuses opened the door to supporting God's work in all sorts of cool ministries around the globe. It was awesome. But a number of years ago, with a struggling start-up business, loss of income, and mounting debt, I stopped giving completely. Everything nonessential was cut, except for our Compassion International kid in Tanzania, Polla.

This wasn't a decision based on anything deeply spiritual—it was about survival. I'm trying to be vulnerable with you right now because I'm hoping you can relate. More importantly, I'm hoping you'll talk candidly with someone you trust about God's role in your finances.

So, let's put the problem squarely on the table: We all live with what I call the *Good Intentions Gap*. It's never more evident than when we talk about money. Our beliefs and our behaviors don't match. Our actions fall woefully short of our aspirations. At the same time, we're desperately hoping for a taste of that glorious freedom we talked about at the beginning of this chapter.

How about you? Are you ready for some freedom?

Good. Before you discuss your LifeSigns results from this section with a friend, let's hear from Jesus himself on how to close the good intentions gap—and find freedom along the way.

THE REAL ISSUE: LORDSHIP

How do you close the gap? How do you turn good intentions into good decisions?

As a practical matter, Dave Ramsey's *Financial Peace University* does a phenomenal job of teaching the "baby steps" to biblical financial freedom, as do the resources available from *Crown Financial Ministries*. We've provided a number of solid resources to help get your financial act together in the second half of this chapter.

As a spiritual matter, let's listen to Jesus, who talked an awful lot about money. Did you know that 40% of Jesus' parables involved money?

In Luke 16, Jesus provides some important and practical instructions about stewardship. When you study scripture, context is critical, so let me quickly set the stage. Jesus has just finished telling the story of the prodigal son, who wasted his father's wealth. In this story, bad stewardship runs headlong into God's grace and produces a truly happy ending. Then, after a tricky parable about a shrewd manager, Jesus delivers the heart of his message on stewardship.

Jesus said, "He who is faithful in a very little thing is faithful also in much; and he who is unrighteous in a very little thing is unrighteous also in much" (Luke 16:10).

Why is Jesus so worked up about the small stuff? Because the little things, easily overlooked or covered up, are a good litmus test of your character. The less people can see you do something, the more it reveals about your heart. Said differently, *HOW you handle money is an indicator of WHO rules your heart*. Little things are big indicators of lordship. That's why Jesus said, "where your treasure is, there your heart will be also" (Matthew 6:21). Bible scholars like to debate which comes first, heart or treasure, but the two definitely go together.

He continues, "Therefore, if you have not been faithful in the use of worldly wealth, who will entrust true riches to you? And if you have not been faithful in the use of that which is another's, who will give you that which is your own?"

Notice that worldly wealth is a steppingstone to "true riches." The way you handle money is a practice field on which God prepares you for bigger things, for eternal things. Jesus is talking about the essence of stewardship.

Little things matter to God.

What's more, chances are it's the little things that kill your budget every month. As a friend often says, "When you're living in North America, it's easy to get nickel and dimed to death." Nobody plans to run out of money before payday, it just happens. The good news is that when you've got a hundred faithful small decisions under your belt, God is going to trust you with some bigger ones.

Finding Freedom in Christ

To our modern, independent way of thinking, this is a bit of a paradox. *Freedom comes from surrender to Christ.*

The apostle Paul beautifully describes how we find freedom in Christ in Galatians chapter five: "It is for freedom that Christ has set us free. Stand firm, then, and do not let yourselves be burdened again by a yoke of slavery" (Galatians 5:1). God's grace had freed the Galatians from following the rules and regulations of Mosaic Law and had freed them to experience the abundant life of Christ.

But make no mistake, *debt is slavery.* Debt is a "law" that demands strict obedience, delivering harsh punishment if not obeyed with timely payments. Debt legally and emotionally binds you to the lender (Proverbs 22:7). So practically speaking, how can the "indwelling Christ" set you free from a life of slavery to Master Card and Visa?

See if you can pick up on Paul's not-so subtle message. According to Galatians 5, as we "walk by the Spirit" and are "led by the Spirit," we can "live by the Spirit" and "keep in step with the Spirit." The result? The Spirit provides you with two major components of good stewardship: faithfulness and self-control.

Paul ends this paradigm-changing chapter about grace and freedom in Christ by saying, *"against such things there is no law"* (Galatians 5:23). When you choose to live in step with the Spirit, who produces faithfulness and self-control in your life, the credit card companies don't stand a chance.

But what if your finances are deep in the red? What if you've been bruised and battered by bad decisions, or a bad economy?

Giving: Starts with Your Heart

The Christians in Macedonia were "extremely poor" and "in the midst of a very severe trial," writes Paul in second Corinthians. We don't know if they faced drought or disease, but it's clear they had very little to offer. Nevertheless, Paul writes, "their overflowing joy and their extreme poverty welled up in rich generosity. For I testify that they gave as much as they were able, and even beyond their ability."

What motivated the generosity of the Macedonians, even as they lived in extreme poverty? Paul writes, "They gave themselves *first of all to the Lord*, and then by the will of God also to us" (2 Corinthians 8:5).

Here's the point: Becoming a good steward doesn't happen just because you've turned over a new leaf. It happens because, like the Macedonians, you've turned your life over to Christ. When you give Him your heart and He frees you from sin, Christ begins to close the gap between your current reality and your true identity. *That's His job, not yours.* Jesus, living in you and through you, is the one who narrows the gulf between your beliefs and behaviors. That includes your finances.

So, here's a very practical question: *Who* is managing your money these days? It is you, or the One who sets you free?

True Stewardship: More than Money

The biblical principle of stewardship applies to much more than your finances. You've probably heard it said you're a steward of everything God has given you, including your time, your talents, and your treasures. Unfortunately, the statistics on serving at my home church almost exactly match those on giving. In case you were wondering, here they are:

> *Approximately 60% of regular attenders only serve "a couple times a year." Forty-five percent don't serve at all.*

Once again, I'll be totally honest with you. I didn't have a single ounce of guilt over being in the 60% who gave less than $100 that year. Why? Because even though I was in survival mode financially, I was still able to gratefully offer the Lord what I did have: my time and my talents.

"Wait a minute, Scott" you say, "does that even count?"

Absolutely. Paul, the apostle, makes it clear, "I urge you, brothers and sisters, in view of God's mercy, to offer your bodies as a living sacrifice, holy and pleasing to God—this is your true and proper worship" (Romans 12:1).

Don't miss the motivation behind the offering: *God's mercy.* You give yourself to God because of grace, not guilt. And notice that God is pleased when you offer your *entire self* as a "living sacrifice." Think about it; that sounds an awful lot like the greatest commandment, doesn't it? Jesus asked you to love Him with all your heart, soul, mind, and strength—not just your checkbook.

Look, you may be upside down on your car loan and drowning in debt. You may be out of work and have little treasure to give. I understand and I've been there too. But what about your time and your talents? For crying out loud, I do corporate surveys and statistics for a living. How on earth could God use someone like that in the church or in the kingdom?

I'll tell you how: He used someone like that to create LifeSigns.

The book you hold in your hands *is* my offering to my church. LifeSigns *is* my living, breathing gift as an "act of worship." If you've read Chapter One of this book, you know that I'm a shining example of struggle, foolishness, and in some cases, outright failure. Do you have any idea how dumbfounded I am that God is willing to live through someone like me? I'm in awe. The only possible explanation is *His outrageous, fantastic, unlimited, amazing grace.*

An Eternal Impact

Think about it this way: Every Sunday, most churches are filled with more raw talent and expertise than a *Fortune 500* company. And according to the LifeSigns stats, 60% of all that experience, 60% of all that wisdom and experience, and 60% of all those unique and wonderful gifts bestowed by the grace of God— *is sitting on the sidelines.*

Conversation Seven – Money and Finances

Meanwhile, the world around us plunges toward an eternity without hope. For years, pastors have been telling us that, "Christ is the hope of the world." And the Spirit-led local church, whether large or small, is the primary way that Jesus helps hurting people.

One pastor put it this way, "There is nothing like the local church when it's working right. Its beauty is indescribable. Its power is breathtaking. Its potential is unlimited. It comforts the grieving and heals the broken in the context of community. It builds bridges to seekers and offers truth to the confused. It provides resources for those in need and opens its arms to the forgotten, the down-trodden, the disillusioned. It breaks the chains of addictions, frees the oppressed, and offers belonging to the marginalized of the world. Whatever the capacity for human suffering, the church has a greater capacity for healing and wholeness. No other organization on earth is like the church. Nothing even comes close."[8]

You don't have to listen to me, but what is the Holy Spirit saying to you right now? When you consider all God has given you in light of eternity, what is the Spirit whispering to your heart? As a good steward, how is God leading you to invest your life differently?

What If . . .

Imagine for a moment what's possible. What if wave after wave of good stewards began to flood every nook and cranny of your local church—every ministry and function—offering themselves as a "living sacrifice?" What if every week dozens of people jammed the church switchboard saying, "Count me in! Where do you need me?"

What if, one year from today, you found yourself more energized and fulfilled than you ever thought possible? It could happen. Remember that God "is able to do immeasurably more

---

[8] Bill Hybels, *Courageous Leadership* (Zondervan, Grand Rapids, Michigan, 2002), p. 23.

than all we ask or imagine, according to His power that is at work within us" (Ephesians 3:20).

Imagine what God could do in your community if an army of fully devoted followers of Christ offered themselves to serve in your neighborhoods, schools, and businesses. Imagine what God could do around the globe with the resources we already have, just waiting in the wings, ready for action.

You see, this chapter really isn't about money.

It's about eternity.

Paul the apostle understood that the stakes are sky-high. He experienced first-hand what Christ could do through a completely redeemed and fully surrendered life. That's why he told the believers in Corinth, "I will most gladly spend and be expended for your souls" (2 Corinthians 12:15).

Can I come right out and say it? As good stewards, it's time to lose the guilt and get in the game with *all that you are in Christ*. That includes your time, your gifts, and yes, your money.

When you do, you'll experience Life like never before.

Are you in?

Conversation Seven – Money and Finances

LifeSign #1: Trusting God for the Future

Financial Security: Being SECURE in God's provision, both now and for the future (knowing God is the ultimate provider, you're trusting Him to meet your needs)

Conversation Starters

What do you think?
1. How's your financial security these days?
2. Do you really trust God? Do you really believe He will provide?
3. Why is it sometimes hard to trust God to provide for you?

Biblical Foundations

What does God say?
- "Therefore I tell you, do not worry about your life, what you will eat or drink; or about your body, what you will wear...Look at the birds of the air; they do not sow or reap or store away in barns, and yet your heavenly Father feeds them. Are you not much more valuable than they? Who of you by worrying can add a single hour to his life?" (Matthew 6:25-27) For context read Matthew 6.
- "Give us each day our daily bread." (Jesus teaching his disciples how to pray in Luke 11:3)

Ideas for Growth

Okay, so now what?
- Consider taking a class like Financial Peace University or Crown Financial. You'll find tons of practical tools, resources, and information to help you manage your finances at DaveRamsey.com.
- Take the step to consult with a professional financial advisor to plan for your future. For a potential list of providers for the services you need go to www.daveramsey.com/elp/

Your Next Step: _____
_____
_____

LifeSigns: How are you? Really.

LifeSign #2: Avoiding Debt

Avoiding Debt: Living BELOW your means (spending less than you make, paying down debt, rather than getting further behind every month)

Conversation Starters

What do you think?
1. According to the Bible, debt is not a sin, but it can be unwise. So how much debt is "too much?"
2. How would your life be different if you were debt free? How would your priorities change?

Biblical Foundations

What does God say?
- "The borrower is slave to the lender." (Proverbs 22:7)
- "The wicked borrow and do not repay, but the righteous give generously." (Psalm 37:21)
- "The Lord will open the heavens, the storehouse of his bounty, to send rain on your land in season and to bless all the work of your hands. You will lend to many nations but will borrow from none." (Deuteronomy 28:12)
- "Let no debt remain outstanding, except the continuing debt to love one another, for whoever loves others has fulfilled the law." (Romans 13:8)

Ideas for Growth

Okay, so now what?
- Keep a log for a week of what you spend your money on. Review it with a spouse or a friend at the end of the week and identify where most of your money is going.
- Consider taking a class like Financial Peace University or Crown Financial. Seek financial counseling for help with financial decision making and budgeting.

Your Next Step: _____
_____
_____

Conversation Seven – Money and Finances

LifeSign #3: Managing Money

Discipline: Taking deliberate steps to MANAGE your money well (knowing where your money goes, planning ahead, so it's not a source of anxiety, distraction, or conflict)

CONVERSATION STARTERS

What do you think?
1. What's your definition of "stewardship?"
2. Can you pinpoint the "budget busters" that find their way into your spending every month?
3. What kind of "system" do you have for managing your money? Is it working?

BIBLICAL FOUNDATIONS

What does God say?
- "The earth is the Lord's, and everything in it, the world, and all who live in it." (Psalm 24:1)
- "Whoever can be trusted with very little can also be trusted with much, and whoever is dishonest with very little will also be dishonest with much." (Luke 16:10) For context read Luke 16.

IDEAS FOR GROWTH

Okay, so now what?
- Read *Managing God's Money* by Randy Alcorn to get a solid foundation of what a good steward looks like in action.
- Have you ever tried the "envelope system" to get on a budget? It's a royal pain in the you-know-what, but it works, especially with an uncooperative spouse or kids.
- Stewardship is more than money. Pray that God would reveal needed changes in how you steward your free time as well.

Your Next Step: _____
_____
_____

LifeSigns: How are you? Really.

LifeSign #4: Making Good Decisions

Good Decisions: Are you able to separate your "wants" from your true "needs?" (seeking God in financial decisions, remembering it ALL belongs to Him – you're just a manager or steward)

Conversation Starters

What do you think?
1. In your opinion, what's the difference between a "want" and a "need?"
2. Given that, how do you typically separate your "wants" from your true "needs?"
3. How can you include God in your financial decisions? Are there specific scriptures you use?

Biblical Foundations

What does God say?
- "I am not saying this because I am in need, for I have learned to be content whatever the circumstances. I know what it is to be in need, and I know what it is to have plenty. I have learned the secret of being content in any and every situation, whether well fed or hungry, whether living in plenty or in want. I can do everything through him who gives me strength." (Philippians 4:11-13)

Ideas for Growth

Okay, so now what?
- If you're married, separating "wants" from "needs" can be a major source of conflict. If that's happening with you, get on the same page by attending a financial class *together*.
- Next time you find something you *really* want, and that you can afford, just walk away (this will hurt). Give it 24 hours and pray about it. See what God does in your heart.

Your Next Step: _____
_____
_____

Conversation Seven – Money and Finances

LifeSign #5: Lifestyle of Contentment

Contentment: Learning to be truly SATISFIED with what you already have (deliberately choosing a simpler lifestyle so you can save, share/give to others)

Conversation Starters

What do you think?
1. Besides your family and kids, what is your single greatest "treasure on earth?" Why?
2. What purpose or cause do you believe in so strongly, that you'd be willing to limit spending in other areas so you could give financially?

Biblical Foundations

What does God say?
- "But, godliness with contentment is great gain. For we brought nothing into the world, and we can take nothing out of it...People who want to get rich fall into temptation and a trap...For the love of money is a root of all kinds of evil. Some people, eager for money, have wandered from the faith and pierced themselves with many griefs." (1 Timothy 6:6-10) For context read 1 Timothy 6.
- "Keep your lives free from the love of money and be content with what you have, because God has said, 'Never will I leave you; never will I forsake you." (Hebrews 13:5)

Ideas for Growth

Okay, so now what?
- Go on a short-term mission trip to a developing country. You'll never look at your lifestyle or a trip to the grocery store the same way again.
- Stand in the middle of your local grocery store and look around. It's incredible. How much of this do you really need to be happy and healthy?

Your Next Step: _____
_____
_____

LifeSigns: How are you? Really.

LifeSign #6: Giving out of Gratitude

Gratitude: Giving to God financially because you really, really WANT to (out of gratitude, rather than a sense of guilt, obligation, or tradition)

Conversation Starters

What do you think?
1. Why do you think Jesus talked so much about money?
2. Which does God want more: your money or your heart? Why?
3. Be honest: When you do give, what's your primary motive? Guilt or gratitude?

Biblical Foundations

What does God say?
- "Remember this: Whoever sows sparingly will also reap sparingly, and whoever sows generously will also reap generously. Each man should give what he has decided in his heart to give...for God loves a cheerful giver. And God is able to make all grace abound to you..." (2 Corinthians 9:6-8)
- "Give, and it will be given to you. A good measure, pressed down, shaken together and running over, will be poured into your lap. For with the measure you use, it will be measured to you." (Luke 6:38)
- "Honor the Lord with your wealth, with the first fruits of all your crops." (Proverbs 3:9)

Ideas for Growth

Okay, so now what?
- Consider reading *The Total Money Makeover: A Proven Plan for Financial Fitness* by Dave Ramsey.
- If you have kids, let them in on your decision-making process around giving. What you give is not as important as WHY you're giving.

Your Next Step: _____
_____
_____

Conversation Eight

Healing and Grace

"The deeper the brokenness, the deeper the growth."
– Pete Briscoe

This question really bothers me: Why didn't God heal Paul?

You may remember the story in the bible. Paul the apostle tells us he was given, "a thorn in my flesh, a messenger of Satan, to torment me" (2 Corinthians 12:7). The Greek word for torment, *kolaphizo*, literally means to "strike with the fist," to treat with "violence or contempt." This thorn wasn't like a splinter in your finger; it was more like a sharp spear in your chest. Whatever it was, Paul was in *physical agony*.

Conversation Eight – Healing and Grace

So, Paul did exactly what you and I would do, "I pleaded with the Lord to take it away from me." You know what happened? Absolutely nothing. In fact, Paul begged God for relief three times. But the thorn did *not* move. God deliberately chose *not* to intervene. Paul's torment continued.

Let's be honest, do you ever wonder, "Why hasn't God fixed me yet?" After all, the Bible says that, "by His wounds we are healed" (1 Peter 2:24). Perhaps you've prayed and waited. You've begged God for relief, and nothing has changed. Your torment continues.

When your desperate prayers for divine intervention go unanswered, two very bad things can happen. First, you can begin to question God's character. I mean, if He's really loving and good, then why does he allow my pain to continue? Second, you can begin to wonder if you're really redeemed by Christ. If you've been set free from the "law of sin and death," then why do you still struggle? Are you really a "new creation," like the scripture says? Or is this some kind of cruel joke?

Those are raw, honest questions. As we tackle the Healing and Grace section of your LifeSigns together, it's critical to move beyond pat answers like: "Just trust and obey," or "Let go and let God," or worse, "If you had more faith, you'd be healed." However well-intentioned, those kinds of clichés hurt more than they help.

So, if you're willing to dig a little deeper, I'd like to explore three biblical reasons why God may choose to leave your thorn in—*and how that could be a good thing.*

Stay with me. Okay?

Reason #1: Learn to Depend on Christ

In 2 Corinthians 12, we discover that something miraculous has happened to Paul. By the power of God, he was, "caught up to paradise and heard things so astounding that they cannot be expressed in words, things no human is allowed to tell" (v 4). God allowed Paul a glimpse of heaven itself. Can you imagine? Paul got a guided tour of the Almighty's maximum security, top-secret realm. Talk about having inside information! What if you somehow traveled to heaven's throne room, had seen the glory of God, and lived to tell the tale? You would never be the same. Well, that's what happened to Paul.

Then Paul tells us, "because of these surpassingly great revelations," and "in order to keep me from becoming conceited, I was given a thorn in my flesh." Another translation says it was, "to keep me from exalting myself."

Okay, that makes sense. After a personal audience with the Master of the universe, Paul could have been poisoned by pride. So, God sent him home with a sure-fire antidote to pride: agonizing, relentless pain. You've been there. You know that suffering is sobering—and humbling. Long-term physical or emotional pain wears you down and drives you to your knees like nothing else. With Paul, I believe God didn't want his beloved apostle to develop an attitude of superiority or independence, just because he'd been to the holy mountain. Said differently, all that heavenly knowledge and insight was never intended to be a *substitute* for Paul's daily dependence on Christ.

His thorn in the flesh made sure of it.

In this context, can you begin to view your chronic struggles or physical suffering in a different light? Could you begin to see your "thorns," not as punishment or neglect, but as a loving Father's daily reminder to depend on Christ? Could this explain why Jesus tells us, "Come to me, all you who are weary and burdened, and I will give you rest?"

Look, I know that lingering physical or emotional pain is exhausting. I've known some very dark places in my life, barren places of utter despair, places where suicide seemed like the only way out. I understand how suffering eats away at the very foundations of your faith. So, I'll say this as gently as possible:

Is it possible that God is more interested in providing you with an intimate relationship, than immediate relief?

Conversation Eight – Healing and Grace

Are you willing to believe that your heavenly Father knows what He's doing, even if you disagree with His methods and timing? I hate waiting—I'll bet you do, too. A quick glance back into the life of David helps put things in perspective.

David penned Psalm 27 in the midst of a horrific, life-threatening situation. Go read it sometime. Not only were people trying to kill him, even his family had forsaken him. That's why I love the way David ends the Psalm with a simple, bold statement of faith: "I would have despaired unless I had believed that I would see the goodness of the Lord in the land of the living. Wait for the Lord; be strong and let your heart take courage; yes, wait for the Lord" (Psalm 27:13-14). David teetered on the brink of despair, but he stubbornly clung to the belief that he would see God's goodness, in God's timing.

Gary Thomas writes, "Waiting, for the believer, is not the futile and desperate act of those who have no other options, but rather a confident trust that eventually God will set things right—even if he is not operating within our preferred time frame."[9]

Here's the point: *Waiting is not punishment, it's preparation.* God is equipping you for your future in ways that rarely make sense in your current situation. Sometimes hindsight is the only source of insight into God's mysterious ways. But for now, learning to depend on Christ, being conformed to the image of Christ, and discovering the riches of intimacy with Christ, will almost always involve . . . waiting.

Reason #2: Relying on God's strength, not yours

God doesn't leave Paul hanging. His painful thorn came with a purpose—and a promise. The Lord's simple response to Paul's pleas gives us hope: "My grace is sufficient for you, for my power is made perfect in weakness" (2 Corinthians 12:9).

---

[9] Gary Thomas, *Authentic Faith* (Zondervan, Grand Rapids, Michigan, 2002), p. 40.

That's a radical equation. *My weakness = His power.* Sometimes, that truth stands in stark contrast to my emotions. Most of my life, I've wrestled with feelings of guilt and shame. For example, when I perform well as a parent, I figure God must be pleased and I feel more confident before Him. But if I "lose it" and raise my voice, wounding my child's spirit, then I feel like a failure. I think, "I haven't changed at all." When that happens, I can start avoiding God, wondering if he's mad at me. All because I don't really understand his grace.

Chuck Swindoll puts it this way, "The only way you qualify to receive His strength is when you admit your weakness, when you admit you're not capable and strong, when, like Paul, you're willing to boast in nothing but your weakness and God's power."[10]

Hear me: *God can and does heal.* Sometimes He removes the thorn and provides glorious relief. On the other hand, your LifeSigns results may describe an affliction that has dogged you for years. What if, despite your best efforts, there's been little sign of progress and you're feeling like a lost cause?

It's time to surrender.

Admit to God that you're wholly, completely unable to fix yourself. Throw yourself before His throne of grace and say, "Lord, I'm finally ready for you to take over." It's not about giving up—but rather looking up. Not just once, but as a new way of life, a life with thorns. You're deliberately moving from despondency to dependency. By faith, firmly plant your foot in Paul's camp and say: "That is why, for Christ's sake, I delight in weaknesses, in insults, in hardships, in persecutions, in difficulties. For when I am weak, then I am strong."

Fun side note: As I write/edit this chapter, it happens to be Christmas morning. Everyone in the house, including the kids, are still asleep. Molly, our six-month-old puppy woke me up at 5:30 AM wanting to go outside. I just found myself shivering in

---

[10] Charles R. Swindoll, *Paul: A Man of Grace and Grit* (The W Publishing Group, Nashville, Tennessee, 2002).

Conversation Eight – Healing and Grace

the backyard, looking up at the sky and saying, "Oh hey God (yawn), Merry Christmas!" That's when He reminded me of a truth that puts all our thorns into perspective: *God is not holding out on you.* He's not a miserly king, hoarding His blessings in tightly clenched fist. Quite the opposite. As I stood in the yard, He brought a wonderful truth to mind: "Remember, He who did not spare His own Son, but gave Him up for us all—how will He not also, along with Christ, graciously give us all things?" (Romans 8:32). Wow. My frustration with my "big issues" evaporates the moment I unwrap God's Christmas gift: His own Son, Jesus.

Reason #3: Comforting Others, as You've Been Comforted

There's no substitute for experience.

The book of 2 Corinthians offers a vivid personal portrait of Paul's suffering: betrayed, persecuted, flogged, beaten, stoned, shipwrecked, constantly in danger, hungry, thirsty, naked—the list of Paul's trials and tribulations in chapter 11 is staggering. So, when Paul opens his letter by talking about God's *comfort*, we'd better sit up, lean forward, and listen. Paul wrote to one church, "I bear on my body the marks of Jesus." This humble man speaks from *deep* personal experience and has the scars on his body to prove it.

Paul begins 2 Corinthians with, "Praise be to the God and Father of our Lord Jesus Christ, the Father of compassion and the God of all comfort, who comforts us in all our troubles…" Don't miss this! "…so that we can comfort those in any trouble with the comfort we ourselves receive from God" (2 Corinthians 1:3-4).

That makes sense. Who better to comfort those facing a divorce, than someone who has walked the painful road of divorce? Who better to help someone recover from an addiction, than one who was once addicted? Who can offer comfort to a victim of sexual abuse better than someone who was also abused? This is one of God's truly magnificent methods for helping hurting people—*by using hurting people.*

I love that about God.

As I've battled with my hurts, habits, and hang-ups over the years, my friend and pastor Eric Willis has often reminded me of this very principle. He'll say, "Scott, your struggles and failures don't disqualify you from ministry, they pre-qualify you."

It's easy to assume that because Christ lives in you, troubles will cease. That's just not true. Shortly before his death, Jesus told his disciples, "In this world you *will* have trouble. But take heart! I have overcome the world" (John 16:33).

Your New Life—Christ Living in You

All your flaws and afflictions, all those scars and addictions, all the stuff you've viewed as the reason why God could never use you, are in fact, the very things that demonstrate God's power to a world without hope. I know this seems counter-intuitive, perhaps because we've come to expect God to "fix us," rather than come and live *through* us.

The late Professor Howard Hendricks was fond of telling aspiring young pastors, "The greatest source of pain in your life will likely become the source of your greatest impact in ministry." Maybe that's one of the reasons why God hasn't "fixed" you yet.

What if God wants you, with all your wounds and failures, to be a living, breathing showcase for His grace?

Finally, take comfort in what Jesus has promised all who trust him as Savior: One day, all your thorns will be removed. It may be today, tomorrow, next year, or it may be when you finally find your way home to heaven. On that day, "He will wipe every tear from their eyes, and there will be no more death or sorrow or crying or pain. All these things are gone forever" (Revelation 21:4).

Paul's earthly life was a showcase for God's grace—thorns and all. And because Paul allowed the power of Christ to be revealed in his weaknesses, the world was never the same.

Conversation Eight – Healing and Grace

You don't have to hide your hurts. By the grace of God, let people see you struggle.

When you do, they'll see your Savior like never before.

LifeSigns: How are you? Really.

LifeSign #1: Sharing your Struggles

Vulnerability: Choosing to REVEAL your struggles to someone you trust (honestly sharing – rather than pretending you're fine, putting on a happy face, hiding your true self)

Conversation Starters

What do you think?
1. Why would you even consider sharing your struggles with another person?
2. Do you have someone you can trust?
3. What would it take for you to be willing to "let someone in" on your stuff?

Biblical Foundations

What does God say?
- "Therefore, confess your sins to each other and pray for each other so that you may be healed. The prayer of a righteous person is powerful and effective." (James 5:16)
- "Carry each other's burdens, and in this way you will fulfill the law of Christ. If anyone thinks they are something when they are not, they deceive themselves." (Galatians 6:2-3)

Ideas for Growth

Okay, so now what?
- One of the names for the Holy Spirit is "Counselor." Start by sharing your heart and struggles with Him.
- Two great books: *Emotionally Healthy Spirituality* by Peter Scazzero and *True Faced* by Bill Thrall.
- Consider mentoring or being mentored by another. Contact your local church and ask for information on mentoring and/or being mentored.
- Get involved with a small group of believers with whom you can grow to be more open and vulnerable.

Your Next Step: _____
_____
_____

Conversation Eight – Healing and Grace

LifeSign #2: Walking Free

Freedom: Successfully AVOIDING things that can hurt or trap you (with the Spirit's power, finding freedom from a hurtful habit like too much food, alcohol, or social media)

CONVERSATION STARTERS

What do you think?
1. Do you have any "hurtful habits?" Are there things you wish you could stop doing?
2. What are some of the best ways you've found to avoid things that can hurt you or trap you?

BIBLICAL FOUNDATIONS

What does God say?
- "A prudent man sees evil and hides himself, the naive proceed and pay the penalty." (Proverbs 27:12)
- "He who walks with wise men will be wise, but the companion of fools will suffer harm." (Prov 13:20)
- "So, if you think you are standing firm, be careful that you don't fall! No temptation has seized you except what is common to man. And God is faithful; he will not let you be tempted beyond what you can bear. But when you are tempted, he will also provide a way out so that you can stand up under it." (1 Corinthians 10:12-13)

IDEAS FOR GROWTH

Okay, so now what?
- This classic has helped many people find freedom: *Hunger for Healing* by Keith Miller.
- Ask friends you trust to hold you accountable in those areas where you struggle. Are there people in your life who pull you down rather than help you grow in Christ? Refrain from putting yourself in positions where you can stumble.

YOUR NEXT STEP: _____
_____
_____

LifeSigns: How are you? Really.

LifeSign #3: Strengths from Struggles

Healing: Discovering how your wounds are HEALED by Christ and how He can use them for good (no longer negatively affecting your life – but now a source of wisdom and strength)

Conversation Starters

What do you think?
1. What's an example of a wound or struggle from your past?
2. How is God using it for good in your life today? What has He taught you? What are you learning about grace?

Biblical Foundations

What does God say?
- "Praise the Lord, O my soul, and forget not all his benefits, who forgives all your sins and heals all your diseases, who redeems your life from the pit and crowns you with love and compassion, who satisfies your desires with good things so that your youth is renewed like the eagle's." (Psalm 103:2-5)
- "And we know that in all things God works for the good of those who love him, who have been called according to his purpose." (Romans 8:28)

Ideas for Growth

Okay, so now what?
- Consider seeing a Christian counselor can help you work through deep wounds and more fully understand how God's grace can transform you.
- Process through one or both of these books: *Connecting* by Larry Crabb or *Life's Healing Choices: Freedom from Your Hurts, Hang-ups, and Habits.*
- Journal your thoughts through a study of *Lord Heal My Hurts* by Kay Arthur.

Your Next Step: _____
_____
_____

Conversation Eight – Healing and Grace

LifeSign #4: Relying on Christ for Strength

Strength: Turning to Jesus as your PRIMARY source of power and hope (relying on God's grace to deal with disappointments, face daily struggles – rather than trying to do it all by yourself)

Conversation Starters

What do you think?
1. Do you have any "thorns?" If so, how have you tried to "fix yourself?"
2. Discuss a time when you truly experienced God's grace and strength in your life. How'd it happen?

Biblical Foundations

What does God say?
- "But he said to me, 'My grace is sufficient for you, for my power is made perfect in weakness.' Therefore, I will boast all the more gladly about my weaknesses, so that Christ's power may rest on me. That is why, for Christ's sake, I delight in weaknesses, in insults, in hardships, in persecutions, in difficulties. For when I am weak, then I am strong." (Paul in 2 Corinthians 12:9-10)
- "Humble yourselves, therefore, under God's mighty hand, that he may lift you up in due time. Cast all your anxiety on him because he cares for you." (1 Peter 5:6-7)
- He himself bore our sins in his body on the tree, so that we might die to sins and live for righteousness; by his wounds you have been healed." (1 Peter 2:24)

Ideas for Growth

Okay, so now what?
- Who can you call, who will really listen to you and would be willing to pray with you?
- Work through the book *Soul Revolution* by John Burke and practice the 60/60 experiment.
- Check out *Hope Again* by Charles Swindoll.

Your Next Step: _____
_____
_____

LifeSign #5: Physical Health

Physical Health: Consistently eating HEALTHY and EXERCISING (so that you have more energy, control your weight, and stay fit and focused)

Conversation Starters

What do you think?
1. Did you know that men are 24% less likely than women to have visited a doctor within the past year? How long has it been for you?
2. If there's one thing you'd change about your diet, what would it be? What about exercise?

Biblical Foundations

What does God say?
- "Do you not know that your bodies are temples of the Holy Spirit, who is in you, whom you have received from God? You are not your own; you were bought at a price. Therefore honor God with your bodies." (1 Corinthians 6:19-20)
- "I discipline my body like an athlete, training it to do what it should." (1 Corinthians 9:27)
- "Each of you should learn to control your own body in a way that is holy and honorable." (1 Thess 4:4)

Ideas for Growth

Okay, so now what?
- In *The Principle of the Path* by Andy Stanley, you'll learn how to break the bad habits, bad behaviors, and bad decisions.
- Check out *Every Body Matters: Strengthening Your Body to Strengthen Your Soul* by Gary Thomas. Proper eating and an active lifestyle can affect how we serve God. The apostle Paul wrote that we need to prime our bodies to become, "an instrument for noble purposes, made holy, useful to the Master and prepared to do any good work."

Your Next Step: _____
_____
_____

Conversation Eight – Healing and Grace

LifeSign #6: Rest and Renewal

Rest and Renewal: Even Jesus needed time to REST after feeding the five thousand. How consistently are you getting down-time to RENEW your mind and body?

CONVERSATION STARTERS

What do you think?
1. When was the last time you truly felt 100% at your best? Physically? Emotionally?
2. Everybody is different: How do you recharge your batteries? What kinds of activities do you find are the most refreshing and renewing to you?

BIBLICAL FOUNDATIONS

What does God say?
- "He gives strength to the weary and increases the power of the weak. Even youths grow tired and weary, and young men stumble and fall; but those who hope in the Lord will renew their strength. They will soar on wings like eagles; they will run and not grow weary; they will walk and not be faint." (Isaiah 40:29-31)
- "Consider it pure joy, my brothers, whenever you face trials of many kinds, because you know that the testing of your faith develops perseverance. Perseverance must finish its work so that you may be mature and complete, not lacking anything." (James 1:2-4) For context read James 1.

IDEAS FOR GROWTH

Okay, so now what?
- On your days off, BE OFF! Don't check emails or go into work. Try spending the time renewing yourself and investing in your family.
- You've heard God's commandment to "remember the Sabbath and keep it holy." But how many of us really observe a Sabbath day of rest?

YOUR NEXT STEP: _____
_____
_____

Conversation Nine

LifeSigns of a Healthy Marriage

*"Yes, your spouse might be difficult to love at times,
but that's what marriage is for—to teach us how to love."*
Gary Thomas,
author of *Sacred Marriage*

Let's be honest. Marriage can be wonderful, but it can also be difficult. Most marriages are a mix of both.

Digging into LifeSigns data from thousands of marriages has yielded a treasure trove of insights. We've identified five major differences between healthy and un-healthy marriages. We've also discovered how marriages evolve over time, and most importantly, what you can do to strengthen yours for the long run. So, let's dig in.

Conversation Nine – Married Life

First, let's look at the current reality. According to recent LifeSigns results, more than one third of married people (37%) sometimes struggle with thoughts of "getting out" when the going gets rough (i.e., being with someone easier, thoughts of separation or divorce). Almost all these people are Christians who regularly attend church, neither of which makes one immune to marriage struggles. Oddly, the ratio of those entertaining thoughts of getting out is about 50% higher for women than for men.

Research by the American Psychological Association and the CDC indicates that healthy marriages can improve mental and physical health, and help children avoid mental, physical, educational, and social problems. A healthy marriage even helps you live longer. Marriage was God's idea, and it's a good one.

You've also heard the statistics: 48% of first marriages, 63% of second marriages, and 71% of third marriages end in divorce. So, let's talk about how you can beat the odds.

"The Dip" – When is the Honeymoon Over?

Common sense tells us that certain seasons of married life are just more difficult than others. LifeSigns data vividly illustrates this fact. We conducted an analysis of marriages across eight different signs of life in marriage:

- Priorities: connecting with your spouse daily
- Decision Making: honoring each other in the process
- Communication: understanding your spouse's heart
- Sex: putting needs of your spouse ahead of your own
- Unity: allowing sex to strengthen your unity as a couple
- Resolving Conflict: working it out with your spouse
- Sticking with it: avoiding thoughts of divorce
- Connecting with Other Couples: sharing what God is teaching you through marriage

While not an exhaustive list of marriage issues, these are some of the biggies. When you compare the overall health of marriages using all eight of these LifeSigns questions (on a scale of 0-100%) against how long people have been married, you can quickly spot "The Dip" in the graph (below).

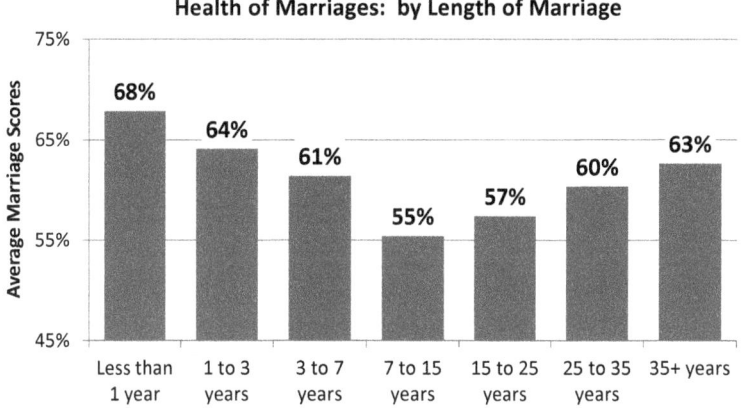

Not surprisingly, most marriages start strong. For couples still in that first year of wedded bliss, LifeSigns scores over 70% are common. However, by the time a couple celebrates their third wedding anniversary, the scores begin to drop. After a couple has been together seven years, we see a significant dip in the health of marriages, with the average falling to 55%.

The honeymoon is definitely over. But why?

For one thing, by the seventh year of marriage, life becomes more complicated. At this point, many couples are raising young kids, paying a mortgage, and juggling demanding careers.

So, what are the implications for your marriage? The middle years will test you. Expect it. The struggle is not the problem; how you deal with the struggle is the problem—and the opportunity. The good news is that a marriage that stands the test of time, also tends to improve over time.

Where is your marriage today? Are you defying the odds? Or are you in the middle of "The Dip?"

Conversation Nine – Married Life

What's Different About Healthy Marriages?

All this LifeSigns data from couples provides a glimpse into what is *different* about people with the healthiest marriages. To learn more, we divided our entire married population into four equally sized groups, based on their average scores for all eight marriage questions:

- Strongest Marriages (83% average marriage score)
- Above Average (67% average marriage score)
- Below Average (53% average marriage score)
- Weakest Marriages (31% average marriage score)

Please understand, we're not judging couples by putting them into these four groups. This is simply a way to explore what's *different* about the *strongest* marriages so we can learn from them.

By comparing people in the strongest marriages with those in the weakest marriages, we've uncovered five major differences that will provide you with some helpful ideas for your marriage. We've listed them in order, from the smallest difference to the largest difference.

Difference #1 – People in healthy marriages have strong non-marital Relationships.

People within the strongest marriages are 43% more likely to say they have non-marital relationships that feel safe where they can "go deep" and "talk about real life." Specifically, they have relationships where it's possible to "be yourself without having to fake it or pretend everything is fine."

No spouse, however delightful and supportive, can meet all your emotional needs. Because God created you to live in community, He often uses relationships *outside* of your marriage to help you learn and grow. That's why isolating from others, especially when you're struggling in marriage, only makes matters worse. The more you feel like you have nowhere to turn, and that no one can relate, the deeper you'll sink into the pit of isolation. It's a vicious cycle.

Can I ask you a personal question? Do you have non-marital relationships that go deep, or do you tend to "put on a happy face" and act like everything is fine? Having a best friend, as you'll see next, is even more important.

Difference #2 – People in healthy marriages have a "best friend."

The book of Proverbs offers a wealth of wisdom about relationships. For example, it says that, "A friend loves at all times. He is there to help when trouble comes" (Proverbs 17:17). And who hasn't experienced times of trouble in marriage?

Our couples in the strongest marriages are 67% more likely to say they have a "best friend" than people in the weakest marriages. In LifeSigns, we describe a best friend as, "someone you've trusted with your struggles and secrets," and "you could call them at midnight, honestly share, and get encouragement."

People in healthy marriages not only have a best friend, but it's the kind of friendship where, "I can tell them anything." This may not sound like the most spiritual definition, but in my experience it's true.

So, here's my next question: *Who can you call at eleven o'clock tonight after an awful fight with your spouse?*

Of course, when you call your friend's cell phone tonight, they'll wonder if somebody has died. But you need someone in your life who will answer that call. You need someone, of the same sex, who will listen to your tale of woe, point you back to Jesus, and still love you in the morning. Do you have that kind of friend? Who comes to mind?

Look again at how Proverbs 17:17 defines friendship. It says a friend is someone who loves "at all times," especially in "a time of trouble." Even at midnight. Even when you've totally blown it with your spouse or have been deeply wounded. People in strong marriages have at least one person who will take that call. Do you?

Conversation Nine – Married Life

Difference #3 – People in healthy marriages are also in a healthy small group.

We're not just talking about any small group. They key factor here is a *healthy* small group. People with the strongest marriages are 140% more likely to be in a healthy small group. Said differently, they're more than twice as likely to be in a small group that is safe, intimate, and willing to doing life together.

As we saw in the chapter on Relationships, getting connected in some form of community is more than a pleasant extra-curricular activity. It's essential to your spiritual health. The same dynamic applies to your marriage. If you've spent much time in a small group, then you know it's filled with people whose marriages are imperfect too. That alone can be encouraging. Believe it nor not, your marriage struggles are not unique. Others are struggling too. So, when members of a group are honest with each other, seeking God's guidance for real marriage issues, positive growth quickly follows.

Difference #4 – People in healthy marriages serve and give.

This one may surprise you. The LifeSigns data shows that those in the strongest marriages are *twice as likely* to serve in ministry on a weekly basis and *three times as likely* to give financially at a level they feel good about. These are large, statistically significant differences. As you'll see, there are good, biblical reasons why giving and serving can strengthen your marriage.

Now, before you tune-out because we're mixing money with a marriage conversation, let me be clear. I'm not suggesting that if you increase your giving or serving that your marriage will miraculously improve overnight. This isn't some kind of magic formula where you give X and get Y. We're also not talking about the overblown claims espoused by "name it and claim it" preachers on late night cable.

That's just silly.

However, the data clearly shows that giving and serving occur much more frequently and consistently in healthy marriages. They go together. A similar correlation is seen between exercise and sleeping better…or sleeping better and exercise. We can't always isolate which one comes first, but we know they go together. The point is, giving and serving are deeply woven into the lives of people who enjoy stronger marriages.

As usual, the Bible sheds some much needed light on this dynamic. Proverbs says, "A generous person will prosper; whoever refreshes others will be refreshed" (Proverbs 11:25). In my experience, serving fills my emotional tank and recalibrates my compass like nothing else. *Serving is a powerful antidote to my natural inclination towards selfishness.* Both serving and giving tend to shift my focus away from my personal issues and toward being more others-oriented, which directly benefits my spouse. And as the verse in Proverbs suggests, serving is downright refreshing. Even Jesus told his disciples that giving will change your heart (Matthew 6:21).

What spouse wouldn't benefit from a mate whose heart is refreshed, renewed, and recalibrated to be more others-oriented?

So, if you're waiting till your marriage is perfect before you get involved and start using your gifts to serve, you may be waiting a very long time. *Instead, see if serving others doesn't teach you how to better serve your spouse.*

Difference #5 – People in healthy marriages talk to other couples about their marriage issues.

"Talk about our marriage issues?" you ask. "Do you mean healthy couples share all their dirty laundry with other couples?"

Not exactly.

Here's what we know: Those in healthy marriages are 500% more likely talk with another couple about what God is teaching them *through marriage*. It's by far the *single largest difference* in

CONVERSATION NINE – MARRIED LIFE

the LifeSigns data between the strongest and weakest marriages (see graph below).

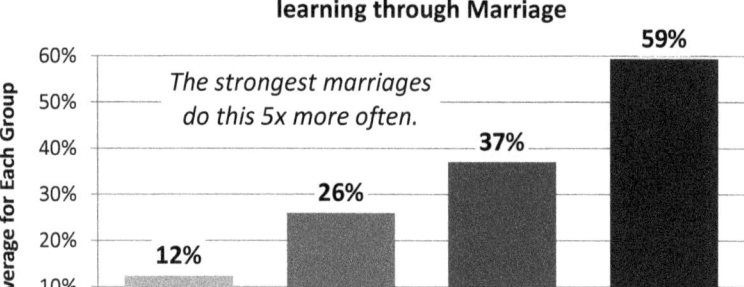

You may remember this question from the Marriage section in LifeSigns. Read it carefully:

Connecting with Other Couples: How regularly are you TALKING with another couple about what God is teaching you through marriage? (i.e., how He's using marriage to reveal your selfishness, to deepen your walk with Christ, and to teach you how to love unconditionally)

I know this is NOT easy. Talking with another couple isn't just the lowest scored LifeSigns question among the eight marriage items, *it's the lowest scored LifeSign of them all.* That's why it's so amazing that people in strong marriages do it 60% of the time. It's radical. It feels unnatural. But it's also vital to the health and protection of your marriage.

As we discussed in Chapter One, the more you hurt, the more you'll tend to hide. But hiding never works.

In the darkest days of my marriage, when we both were feeling wounded and defeated, the *last thing* we wanted to do was share our junk with the lovely couple who had joined us for dinner and a movie. So we didn't. Yet, over the years, we found ourselves sitting across the kitchen table with a handful of mature, Godly couples, sharing our painful story and learning from theirs.

"Big deal," you say, "a little coffee and conversation with another couple sounds lovely. We do this all the time."

Not so fast.

Listen, if you're going to talk about real marriage issues, this is much harder than it sounds. You're literally going to trust another couple with some of the most private, sensitive issues in your life. This kind of candid conversation can make a grown man run for cover. But it's through dozens of these difficult conversations that I've stumbled into a good rule of thumb for all of marriage: *When in doubt, humble myself.*

Believe me, talking with another couple about what's really happening in your marriage is humbling. I have literally bitten my lip until it bled as my mate talked about my shortcomings as a husband with another couple. But Peter reminds us that, "God is opposed to the proud, but *gives grace to the humble*" (1 Peter 5:5). Becoming known to another couple frees you from the prison of isolation and opens the floodgates of God's grace. Plus, it allows another couple to learn from your experiences, to hold you accountable, and to share what they're learning through marriage. It's a win-win scenario.

So, here's one more nosey question: *What would it take for you and your spouse to have this type of candid conversation with another couple? Who would you ask?*

Notice the theme running through all this LifeSigns data: People in strong marriages have the opportunity to talk about marriage with other couples more frequently, simply because they're plugged into a healthy, safe, and supportive small group. That's yet another reason to find a church and get plugged in.

Clearly, a small group can be much more than a social gathering to grill burgers and talk about your kids (not that there's anything wrong with that). If you're willing to go further, to dig

Conversation Nine – Married Life

deeper, and to share real-life marriage issues with another couple, it could make all the difference in the health and longevity of your marriage. Just be sure to read and follow the helpful guidelines in Chapter Three: A Candid Conversation Guide.

The Bottom Line: Implications for Your Marriage

The reality for most of us is this: a healthy, intimate marriage just doesn't happen by osmosis. And don't believe the myth that if you can just find the right person, a soul mate, then you'll automatically experience wedded bliss, free from conflict or pain. That's not realistic. Whether your spouse is highly compatible or not, a strong marriage is the product of focused time and effort, close non-marital relationships, and genuine humility, all grounded in the redeeming work of Christ.

There are probably a hundred things that contribute to an intimate, healthy marriage. What's more, the mix of important factors varies from one couple to the next. But across thousands of marriages, the latest LifeSigns data points to five characteristics of healthy couples. In summary, people in the strongest marriages:

- are 43% more likely to have authentic non-marital relationships where they can go deep
- are 67% more likely to have a best friend
- are 140% more likely to be in a healthy small group
- are 200-300% more likely to serve and give regularly
- are 500% more likely to talk with another couple about what God is teaching them through marriage

Look beyond the stats and figures for a minute. Each of these items represents a practical step you can take to strengthen your marriage. Don't miss the fact that four out of five of these areas will improve when you've plugged into a small, tightly knit group of friends.

LIFESIGNS: HOW ARE YOU? REALLY.

My pastor is fond of saying, "We don't want anyone to do life alone." To which we should add, "don't do marriage alone either."

IMPORTANT: CONVERSATION STARTERS

The conversation starters on the pages that follow include some relevant and challenging questions to facilitate an honest dialogue with your spouse, or with a small group. Don't forget to use your LifeSigns Growth Plan, since it already includes your top priority and your greatest struggle from the Marriage section.

Warning: If you're having a candid conversation about marriage in a small group, *we strongly recommend that you split up into groups of men and women.* Why? In my experience it's easier and safer to discuss these issues in a same-sex group, without your spouse glaring at you from across the room. Once you've had your separate discussions, come back together and debrief as couples.

Small Group Leaders: Be sure to check out *Chapter Three: A Candid Conversation Guide* for some proven and practical guidelines on how to facilitate grace-filled conversations. That's a nice way of saying, "This thing can get horribly messy if you don't handle it properly." I speak from experience. Have a game plan, lay down some basic ground rules, and keep a firm hand on the conversation. When you do, people will feel safe and good things will happen with the couples in your group.

An excellent resource on how to have safe, productive conversations is called the "Speaker/Listener Technique."

Speaker/Listener Technique:
marriagemissions.com/speaker-listener-technique

Conversation Nine – Married Life

LifeSign #1: Connecting with your Spouse

Your Priorities: How often do you truly CONNECT with your spouse on a DAILY basis? (not just talking about the schedule or juggling errands, but intimately engaging with one another)

Conversation Starters

What do you think?
1. What does "connecting" with your spouse mean to you? Be specific.
2. What gets in the way of connecting?
3. How can you ensure you connect on a daily basis? How can you make it a priority?

Biblical Foundations

What does God say?
- "Show me your face, let me hear your voice; for your voice is sweet, and your face is lovely." (Song of Solomon 2:14)
- "You have stolen my heart, my sister, my bride; you have stolen my heart with one glance of your eyes." (Song of Solomon 4:9)
- "The man said; 'This is now bone of my bones and flesh of my flesh; she shall be called woman, for she was taken out of man." (Genesis 2:23)

Ideas for Growth

Okay, so now what?
- Grab the remote, turn off the TV, look your mate in the eye and ask this person you've married, "How are you? Really." Now listen!
- Read *Night Light* by Dr. James Dobson, or *Love Talk* by Les and Leslie Parrott in order to brush up on how to connect.
- Schedule a regular date night with your spouse. If you have kids, find another couple with kids and take turns watching the kids. The kids will love hanging out and you don't have to pay a babysitter!

Your Next Step: _____

_____

_____

LifeSigns: How are you? Really.

LifeSign #2: Making Decisions with Grace

Decision-making: Consistently HONORING one-another when making decisions (whether it's a big decision about finances or parenting, or a small one, like deciding where to go for dinner)

Conversation Starters

What do you think?
1. What kinds of decisions are difficult, or cause conflict in your relationship?
2. How can you honor your spouse through the decision-making process?
3. In your opinion, what does it mean to be "easily persuaded?"

Biblical Foundations

What does God say?
- "Therefore, as God's chosen people, holy and dearly loved, clothe yourselves with compassion, kindness, humility, gentleness and patience." (Colossians 3:12)
- "Submit to one another out of reverence for Christ." (Ephesians 5:21)
- "Let your conversation be always full of grace." (Colossians 4:6)
- Also see the whole chapter of Ephesians 5.

Ideas for Growth

Okay, so now what?
- A good resource on learning to communicate and collaborate as a couple is *Fighting for Your Marriage* by Howard Markham.
- Consider how you can honor each other's opinions and desires, even when you disagree.
- A great book for any marriage is *Love and Respect* by Emerson Eggerichs.

Your Next Step: _____
_____
_____

CONVERSATION NINE – MARRIED LIFE

LifeSign #3: Listening with your Heart

Communication: Learning to truly UNDERSTAND your spouse's heart (you honor the feelings behind an issue—even when you do not agree or it's not "logical")

CONVERSATION STARTERS

What do you think?
1. What's the difference between *listening* and *understanding*?
2. How well do you understand your spouse's heart behind the words?
3. How well do you feel understood by your mate?

What does God say?

BIBLICAL FOUNDATIONS

- "A fool finds no pleasure in understanding, but delights in airing his own opinions." (Proverbs 18:2)
- "The purposes of a man's heart are deep waters, but a man of understanding draws them out." (Proverbs 20:5)
- "Everyone should be quick to listen, slow to speak and slow to become angry, for man's anger does not bring about the righteous life that God desires." (James 1:19-20)

Okay, so now what?

IDEAS FOR GROWTH

- Study your spouse. Become an expert at how God has uniquely wired them and how they communicate. It will help. A lot.
- Find another couple who seem to communicate well. Get together and ask lots of questions about how they relate to and understand each other.
- Read and discuss one of these books: *The Five Love Languages* by Gary Chapman, *Love Talk* by Drs. Les and Leslie Parrott, or *Love and Respect* by Emerson Eggerichs.

Your Next Step: _____
_____
_____

LifeSigns: How are you? Really.

LifeSign #4: Practicing Selfless Sex

Selfless Sex: Putting the needs of your spouse AHEAD of your own (adopting a servant's heart—whether you're the one who wants to have sex—or the one who would rather not)

Conversation Starters

What do you think?
1. Why did God put sex into marriage? Seriously. Answer this one first.
2. If you viewed sex as an act of *service*, how would that change your approach and mindset? Be specific, but not graphic.
3. How can you cultivate a "servant's heart" in the bedroom?

Biblical Foundations

What does God say?
- "Now that I, your Lord and Teacher, have washed your feet, you also should wash one another's feet. I have set you an example…" (John 13:14-15a)
- "Your attitude should be the same as Christ Jesus… (who) made Himself nothing, taking the very nature of a servant." (Philippians 2:5-7)
- "The husband should fulfill his marital duty to his wife, and likewise the wife to her husband." (1 Corinthians 7:3)
- Turn to 1 Corinthians 7:4-5 for more on selfless sex.

Ideas for Growth

Okay, so now what?
- In private, ask your spouse: "How can I better serve you when it comes to our physical relationship?" Listen, ask questions, and take good notes.
- Listen to and discuss the *Song of Solomon* audio series by Tommy Nelson, Denton Bible Fellowship.
- Read *His Needs, Her Needs: Building an Affair-Proof Marriage*, by Willard F. Jr. Harley. Very practical.

Your Next Step: _____
_____
_____

Conversation Nine – Married Life

Important Considerations on LifeSigns #4 & 5

Marriage LifeSign #4 – Practicing Selfless Sex:
By asking a LifeSigns question about "selfless-sex," we may be hitting a raw nerve or deep wound. I understand that sex is a highly personal issue and there are often strong feelings associated with it. So first, let's acknowledge that any number of things can prevent a married couple from being sexually active: age, disability, military service, past wounds or abuse, infidelity, side-effects from medications, as well as couples who are separated but still married.

Second, if the topic of sex sets off flashing lights and warning sirens in your heart and mind, I'd strongly encourage you to read *Conversation Eight: Healing and Grace* in this book. And please remember this simple truth: "The Lord is close to the broken-hearted and saves those who are crushed in spirit" (Psalm 34:18). God's abundant grace flows freely into every area of our lives, including our marital sexuality.

Marriage LifeSign #5 – Sex and Unity:
In asking about "sex and unity," we may be hitting another raw nerve. Obviously, marital unity is about *much more* than physical intimacy; it's also about honest communication, mutual respect, an emotional connection, and other factors. Nevertheless, we're asking this question because sex can also be a source of conflict and pain in marriage. It's better to get the issues on the table so you can address them, instead of avoiding them.

That said, if you are facing physical or emotional abuse, adultery, addiction to pornography, or any other destructive behavior in your marriage, please reach out to a pastor, friend, or qualified counselor. Please put down the book and make that call right now. You do not have to allow a hurtful or damaging situation to continue. Take a step of faith and ask for help.

Okay?

LifeSigns: How are you? Really.

LifeSign #5: Sex and Unity

Unity through Intimacy: How often do you feel sex strengthens your UNITY as a couple? (rather than a source of conflict, tension, division, or pain in your relationship)

Conversation Starters

What do you think?
1. In your marriage, does sex tend to draw you closer together emotionally or drive you farther apart?
2. What issues *outside* the bedroom affect your physical intimacy?
3. How can sex be more of a unifying force in your relationship?

Biblical Foundations

What does God say?
- "For this reason, a man will leave his father and mother and be united to his wife, and they will become one flesh." (Genesis 2:24)
- "Do not deprive each other except by mutual consent and for a time, so that you may devote yourselves to prayer. Then come together again so that Satan will not tempt you." (1 Corinthians 7:5)
- "May you rejoice in the wife of your youth…may you ever be captivated by her love." (Proverbs 5:18-19)
- "Marriage should be honored by all, and the marriage bed kept pure." (Hebrews 13:4)

Ideas for Growth

Okay, so now what?
- In private, ask your spouse: "Is there anything about our physical relationship I need to know, that you've been reluctant to tell me?"
- Read *A Celebration of Sex: A Guide to Enjoying God's Gift of Sexual Intimacy* by Douglas E. Rosenau.

Your Next Step: _____

_____

_____

Conversation Nine – Married Life

LifeSign #6: Resolving Conflict

Resolving Conflict: When there's an issue, consistently trying to resolve it that SAME DAY (discuss and reconcile, rather than go to bed angry or hurt, with the issue unresolved)

Conversation Starters

What do you think?
1. Disagreement is a part of marriage. When a conflict escalates, do you typically respond with *fight* or *flight*? How does that look for you?
2. By comparison, when you're handling conflict in a healthy, productive way, what is *different*?
3. What's the most important thing you've learned about resolving conflict with your spouse?

Biblical Foundations

What does God say?
- "In your anger do not sin: Do not let the sun go down while you are still angry, and do not give the devil a foothold." (Ephesians 4:26)
- "A gentle answer turns away wrath, but a harsh word stirs up anger." (Proverbs 15:1)
- "Husbands, love your wives and do not be harsh with them." (Colossians 3:19)
- "Above all, love each other deeply, because love covers over a multitude of sins." (1 Peter 4:8)
- Also see all of 1 Peter 3.

Ideas for Growth

Okay, so now what?
- Work through one of these good books with your spouse: *Fighting for Your Marriage* by Markman, Stanley, and Blumberg or *Resolving Everyday Conflict* by Kevin Johnson and Ken Sande.
- Talk with another couple whom you respect. Ask them to share how they've learned to resolve conflict in a way that honors God and each other.

Your Next Step: _____
_____
_____

LifeSigns: How are you? Really.

LifeSign #7: Protecting your Marriage

Staying at it: When you two struggle—and every couple does—do you DISCARD any thoughts of getting out of marriage? (avoiding fantasies of being with someone easier or thoughts of divorce)

Conversation Starters

What do you think?
1. See the scriptures below: Why does God want you to "guard your heart" and "take captive" your thoughts? Especially when it comes to bailing out of your marriage?
2. When the going gets tough, how are you able to *protect* your heart and mind from lingering on thoughts of getting out of your marriage?

What does God say?

Biblical Foundations

- "Above all else, guard your heart, for everything you do flows from it." (Proverbs 4:23)
- "We take captive every thought to make it obedient to Christ." (2 Corinthians 10:5)
- "Bear with each other and forgive whatever grievances you may have against one another. Forgive as the Lord forgave you. And over all these virtues put on love, which binds them all together in perfect unity." (Colossians 3:12-14)

Okay, so now what?

Ideas for Growth

- Need a fresh start? Check out a marriage intensive retreat, like at the Center for Relational Care at www.relationalcare.org.
- Chapter by chapter, read and discuss the book *Sacred Marriage* by Gary Thomas with your spouse. Gary asks a truly profound question: "What if God designed marriage to make us Holy, more than to make us happy?"

Your Next Step: _____

_____

_____

Conversation Nine – Married Life

LifeSign #8: Connecting with other Couples

Connecting with Other Couples: Regularly TALKING with another couple about what God is teaching you through marriage? (how He is using marriage to challenge your selfishness, to deepen your walk with Jesus, to teach you how to love unconditionally)

Conversation Starters

What do you think?
1. Why did the LifeSigns research show that people in the strongest marriages also have healthy relationships *outside* of marriage?
2. What are the potential benefits of talking *honestly* with another couple about your marriage stuff?
3. What prevents you, as a couple, from connecting deeply with another couple about marriage issues?

Biblical Foundations

What does God say?
- "When we get together, I want to encourage you in your faith, but I also want to be encouraged by yours." (Romans 1:12)
- "Carry each other's burdens, and in this way you will fulfill the law of Christ." (Galatians 6:2)
- "Consider how we may spur one another on toward love and good deeds. Let us not give up meeting together, as some are in the habit of doing, but let us encourage one another—and all the more as you see the Day approaching." (Heb 10:24-25)

Ideas for Growth

Okay, so now what?
- Go on a double date with another couple and ask "So what's God teaching you through your marriage?" Be ready to share what you're learning.
- Find a couples retreat or marriage conference to attend. It will provide a safe way for you to talk with other couples about marriage issues.

Your Next Step: _____
_____
_____

Conversation Ten

The LifeSigns of Parenting

"Train up a child in the way he should go—but be sure you go that way yourself."
– Charles H. Spurgeon

I t's easy to worry about your kids.

After all, the very first family started out with two perfect children (Adam and Eve), the perfect environment (the garden), with the perfect parent (God himself). The kids were raised with unconditional love, unrestricted access to their Father, and unlimited resources. This was the very definition of a "best case scenario" for raising obedient, well-adjusted children.

How did they turn out? *They rebelled.*

Conversation Ten – Parenting

In my experience, parenting can be difficult, is often baffling, and yet it can be tremendously rewarding. Yes, you have a God-ordained responsibility to train and nurture your children. Yes, you need to set appropriate boundaries, provide correction when needed, and give your kids a solid understanding of the redeeming work of Jesus Christ. It's all important.

And despite your best efforts, they may still rebel. *It's called "free will."*

As you've discovered, your kids don't function like your computer, accepting your input and executing your commands. That would be nice. To correct aberrant behavior, you'd just install an update to their operating system and hit re-boot. No, the reality is one moment your kids are obedient lambs and you're the wise shepherd. The next minute, they're wild animals and you're the overwhelmed zookeeper. What's more, kids can exercise their free will at the worst possible moments (i.e., at the grocery store, on a family vacation, or when you have friends over for dinner).

Unfortunately, there's no magic bullet. Like you, I'm in the trenches every day, battling an endless to-do list and trying to raise two good kids in the process. Some days, success with the kids amounts to survival—rather than anything deeply spiritual.

I can offer some surprising results from the latest batch of LifeSigns data about what works, and what isn't working. We've collected data from thousands of parents, just like you, who are trying to raise good kids.

We uncovered some key differences between parents with kids who are doing well, and parents with kids that are struggling. Our research answers two questions: (1) What positively or negatively influences our kids to follow Christ? (2) What is different about parents with kids who are doing well, when compared to those who are not.

Also, as you prepare to review your LifeSigns results from the Parenting section, remember we've compiled a number of excellent resources at the back of this chapter.

LifeSigns: How are you? Really.

Insight #1: Who, or What, influences your kids most?

Parenting is largely an influence job. You don't have total control and they have free will. Which begs the question: "What influences your children most?" First, we need to set the stage. The parenting section of your LifeSigns assessment covered a half-dozen key issues related to raising good kids, including:

- Communication: encouraging your kids to openly share their struggles, fears, and dreams with you
- Teaching Truth: helping your kids to discuss and apply scripture to everyday life
- Discipline: addressing the underlying heart and motives, not just the behavior
- Following Christ: encouraging your kids to deliberately follow Jesus, not just go with the flow
- Being an Example: consistently modeling how to live by faith for your kids
- Purpose: encouraging your kids to live for something bigger than themselves

You may remember that we asked how often these signs of life are true for your children, according to your most recent experience. *The focus of these six questions was primarily on your kids, not you.*

We averaged together responses to the six parenting items to create a composite index that ranges from 0-100%. In order to make comparisons between children who are doing well and those who are struggling, we divided the population into three roughly equal size groups:

- Kids "doing well" (upper 1/3)
- Kids "doing okay" (middle 1/3)
- Kids that are "struggling" (bottom 1/3)

Conversation Ten – Parenting

Please understand, we're not judging these children or their parents by putting them into these three groups. This is simply a way to uncover what's different about children who are "doing well" so that we can identify ways to raise good kids.

Still with me? Now for the big question: *What's different about kids who are doing well? What influences them most?*

Understanding the Influences

The top two influences in the lives of kids who are "doing well" are: (1) parents and (2) the family unit. In stark contrast, kids who are struggling are primary influenced by their peers, including school friends, kids on the block, sports teams, etc.

Consider the implications. Parents with kids who are struggling are *not* the primary influence in their children's lives—it's *their friends*. We know that peer pressure is powerful. In the case of kids who are struggling, someone other than the parent holds sway over the child's heart and mind. And that "someone" is likely under the age of 18 and may have a completely different set of values from the kid's parent.

Here's the list of the five strongest influences for kids *doing well*:
  #1 – parents
  #2 – the family unit
  #3 – friends and peers
  #4 – Jesus Christ and the Bible
  #5 – youth groups, church friends, coaches, camp counselors

Now look at the five greatest influences of *struggling* kids:
  #1 – friends and peers
  #2 – parents and family
  #3 – television, movies, music, media, etc.
  #4 – social media, internet activity (Facebook, Instagram)
  #5 – gaming (Xbox, PlayStation, Wii, on-line multiplayer)

Those are two very different lists. Except for the influence of friends and family in both groups, everything else is different. For kids doing well, we find the strong influence of Jesus Christ and scripture, plus youth groups, coaches, and church friends. That sharply contrasts with what influences kids who are struggling: TV and movies, social media, gaming, and the internet.

While I'm sorely tempted to climb atop my soapbox and rail against the potentially negative influences of too much television, social media, and gaming on a child's development, I won't. You can draw your own conclusions.

Plus, there's more to this story.

When comparing all 13 sources of influence measured in LifeSigns, we were not trying to make a spiritual statement. Candidly, this section of LifeSigns was a more of a "fishing expedition." We wanted to understand the biggest differences between kids who are healthy versus those who are struggling. It could have been anything. But when we crunched the numbers, Jesus and the Bible stood out. (Meaning, it had the most statistically significant correlation).

The bottom line: *No other source of influence comes close to the difference made by "Jesus Christ and the Bible"* (below).

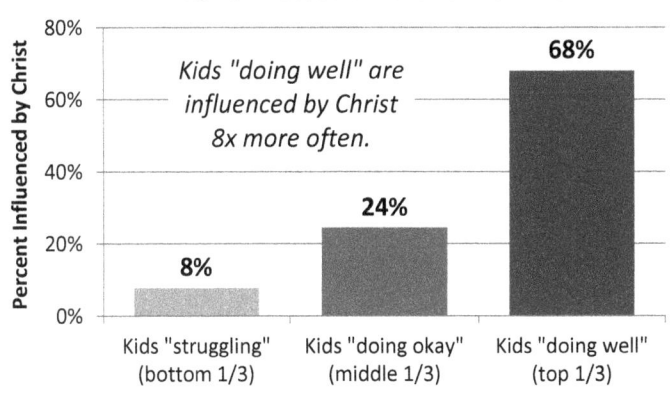

Conversation Ten – Parenting

Some observations are in order. First, not every parent with kids who are "doing well" said that Jesus and the Bible are among the top three influences, but the vast majority of them did (almost 70%). Second, don't miss the *magnitude* of the difference between the kids doing well versus kids who are struggling. Kids who are primarily influenced by "Jesus and the Bible" are *eight times more likely* to be among those who are doing well. That's an 800% difference.

Too many statistics? Then let me try to put this into a compact headline:

TO RAISE GODLY KIDS, YOU NEED GOD'S INFLUENCE.

Think about it. Can you single-handedly compete with the 24/7 juggernaut of television, social media, and internet, all mixed together with constant peer pressure in our highly secular culture? No, you're probably going to lose that battle.

Here's the good news. We parents have an ally far more powerful than all those forces combined: *the living Word of God*. I don't know about you, but I rarely think of Jesus as "the living Word." He's more like a savior and friend. But in describing Jesus, the gospel of John opens by telling us, "the Word became flesh and made his dwelling among us" (John 1:14). Hebrews goes even further in telling us that God's word is, "living and active," filled with divine power to penetrate deeply into the "thoughts and attitudes of the heart" (Hebrews 4:12). That sounds like a powerful source of influence to me!

When your kids are infused with God's word, they've got more than just biblical truth on their side, *they're being actively influenced by God himself.*

So, pause and honestly consider: Who, or what, influences your children the most these days? If you're not sure, here are a few helpful questions: How do my kids spend free time? Who do they hang out with? What media do they consume when I'm not looking? Most importantly, how much of God's powerful, living, and active Word is hidden in their heart? As we're reminded in Psalm 119, "How can a young person stay on the path of purity? By living according to your word" (v. 9).

LifeSigns Insights #2: What's different about You?

Once we started comparing kids who are doing well with those that are struggling, the logical next step was to look for differences between the parents themselves. Let me just say, I know these are treacherous waters. Correlating your personal LifeSigns scores with those related to your children, is by definition, meddling in a sensitive area. So, let's make a deal: I'll share the results of the research and leave the discussion of how it might apply to you personally for your horizontal conversation with someone you trust.

The basic question is this: What's different about *the parents* of kids who are doing well? Without getting too technical, we used a variety of reliable statistical methods to identify the top ten things that make a real difference in the children's scores. (In case you were wondering, we used stratification, correlation, multiple-regression, and significance testing).

Headline #1: Here's the first surprise. The biggest difference between the parents of kids doing well and kids who struggle is an item from the section on Work Life:

> *Time – Effectively balancing your work demands with the rest of your life (i.e., business travel, family life, project deadlines, etc.).*

In other words, how well a parent handles the demands placed on their time by work has the strongest positive relationship to how well their kids are doing at home. With both parents working in many families, and especially for single parents, it turns out that

CONVERSATION TEN – PARENTING

the daily juggling act is, in fact, a major contributor to your children's spiritual health.

HEADLINE #2: Here's the second surprise. We found that five of the top ten areas in the lives of parents with kids doing well all related to the gospel of Christ. These parents are more consistently reaching out to non-Christians, living differently than the rest of the world, becoming others-oriented, sharing with others at the Spirit's nudge, and developing confidence in answering questions about the gospel. Said differently, *parents who frequently share Christ with others, also have kids who more frequently follow Christ.*

HEADLINE #3: It's not surprising that two marriage items bubbled to the top of our list. These included (1) connecting with another couple to talk about what God is teaching you through marriage, and (2) truly understanding your spouse's heart (through more effective communication). This confirmed our suspicions: Kids raised in the context of a healthy marriage really are doing better across the board.

HEADLINE #4: It's interesting to note that *none* of the items related to Money and Finances showed a statistically significant relationship to the kids' scores. Money issues didn't even make the Top 10 list.

SO WHAT?

You may point out, "There are dozens of things that contribute to my children's growth and well-being." That's true. The latest LifeSigns research only includes 54 of them. On the other hand, all of those 54 LifeSigns were drawn directly from scripture, so they shouldn't be ignored.

As a chronically busy business owner, I'm squirming in my chair when I learn that balancing my time at work with time at home is the number one LifeSign associated with my children's well-being. I'll bet you've found the daily balancing act to be challenging too.

I'm also pondering the connection between sharing Christ *outside* my family and having kids who follow Christ *inside* my family. There's something profound about that correlation, but I'm not sure that I fully understand it yet. Maybe knowing and sharing the gospel is more important to raising Godly kids than we suspect?

Now what?

As you review your LifeSigns results from the Parenting section, flip back through your profile to see how you're doing with the items above that make the biggest difference in the spiritual health of your children. Then make your own connections.

And ask yourself, "How does my relationship with Christ, influence my kids' relationship with Jesus?" Can you confidently say to your kids, as Paul the apostle said to his spiritual children in Corinth, "Be imitators of me, just as I also am of Christ?" (1 Corinthians 11:1).

Your kids are watching you—more than you realize. Let them see you how you love and follow Jesus with your whole heart.

As you follow Christ, chances are, they will too.

Conversation Ten – Parenting

LifeSign #1: Connecting with your Kids

Communication: Encouraging your kids OPENLY share their struggles, fears, and dreams with you (because you've created a safe environment—rather than being "on the outside looking in")

Conversation Starters

What do you think?
1. Communication: What's the best way you've found to get your kids to openly share their thoughts and feelings with you?
2. What about your parents? What was it like growing up? Safe? Shallow? Supportive? Combative?
3. Do your kids trust you not to try to "fix them?" How difficult is it for you to really listen *before* you offer direction or guidance?

Biblical Foundations

What does God say?
- "The purposes of a man's heart are deep waters, but a man of understanding draws them out." (Proverbs 20:5)
- "These commandments that I give you today are to be upon your hearts. Impress them on your children..." (Deuteronomy 6:6-7)

Ideas for Growth

Okay, so now what?
- Try some low-tech time together: One night, turn off the television, computers, and phones. Play a board or card game together; enjoy laughing and talking as a family. Ordering pizza is optional.
- Understanding your child's "love language" will open up opportunity for authentic and consistent communication.
- Read *The Five Love Languages of Children* by Gary Chapman & Ross Campbell. It's loaded with practical ways to understand and affirm your kids.

Your Next Step: _____
_____
_____

LifeSigns: How are you? Really.

LifeSign #2: Teaching Truth

Teaching Truth: Encouraging your kids to discuss and APPLY the Bible to their life (beyond a family devotional, helping them to explore what God has to say about issues they face)

Conversation Starters

What do you think?
1. When it comes discussing scripture, what's the difference between *teaching* and *sharing*?
2. When was the last time you shared with your kids how you've applied God's Word to *your life*?
3. How does "connecting with your kids" affect your ability to "teach truth?" How are the two related?

Biblical Foundations

What does God say?
- "Fix these words of mine in your hearts and minds; tie them as symbols on your hands and bind them on your foreheads." (Deuteronomy 11:18)
- "Teach them to your children, talking about them when you sit at home and when you walk along the road, when you lie down and when you get up." (Deuteronomy 11:19)
- "All Scripture is God-breathed and useful for teaching, rebuking, correcting and training in righteousness, so that the man of God may be thoroughly equipped for every good work." (2 Timothy 3:16-17)

Ideas for Growth

Okay, so now what?
- Let your kids "catch you" reading your Bible. And when you're struck by something in scripture, share it with them. Ask what they think. Listen.
- A family's influence on a child is 2-3 times stronger than church. See *Faith Begins at Home* by Mark Holeman or *Age of Opportunity*, Paul David Tripp.

Your Next Step: _____
_____
_____

CONVERSATION TEN – PARENTING

LIFESIGN #3: SHEPHERDING THE HEART

Discipline: When your kids mess up, how consistently do they RESPOND to correction in a positive way? (with genuine repentance—a change of heart and mind, not just behavior)

CONVERSATION STARTERS

What do you think?
1. Quick Case Study: What is the number one behavioral issue you're facing with your kids?
2. Now, what's going on in you son or daughter's *heart* behind the behavior? Can you pinpoint the real spiritual issue here?
3. Now the hardest part, how do you address *both* your kid's behavior and their *heart/motives*?

What does God say?
- "Above all else, guard your heart, for everything you do flows from it." (Proverbs 4:23)
- "Listen, my sons, to a father's instruction; pay attention and gain understanding. I give you sound learning, so do not forsake my teaching" (Proverbs 4:1-2)
- "Fathers, do not exasperate your children." (Ephesians 6:4)

BIBLICAL FOUNDATIONS

IDEAS FOR GROWTH

Okay, so now what?
- Do you know what motivates your child? Each kid is unique and responds to correction differently. If your approach isn't working, adapt to address the heart, not just the behavior.
- Book suggestions: *Shepherding a Child's Heart* by Ted Tripp will revolutionize how you approach parenting children of all ages. Also see *Boundaries with Kids* by Dr. Henry Cloud & Dr. John Townsend for incredibly helpful, biblical advice.

YOUR NEXT STEP: _____

_____

_____

LifeSigns: How are you? Really.

LifeSign #4: Following Jesus

Life with Jesus: Are your children deliberately CHOOSING to follow Jesus Christ? (getting ownership of their faith, not just going with the flow)

CONVERSATION STARTERS

What do you think?
1. How old were you when your relationship with Christ became *yours*? How did it happen for you?
2. Do your kids really "own" their faith? Or are they just following the crowd?
3. Besides going to church or youth group, how can you encourage your kids to know and follow Jesus?

BIBLICAL FOUNDATIONS

What does God say?
- "From this time many of His disciples turned back and no longer followed Him. 'You do not want to leave too, do you?' Jesus asked the Twelve. Simon Peter answered him, 'Lord, to whom shall we go? You have the words of eternal life.'" (John 6:66-68)
- "For you have been my hope, O Sovereign Lord, my confidence since my youth. Since my youth, O God, you have taught me, and to this day I declare your marvelous deeds." (Psalm 71:5, 17)
- "I have hidden your word in my heart, that I might not sin against you." (Psalm 119:11)

IDEAS FOR GROWTH

Okay, so now what?
- Interview your kids. In an age appropriate way, ask them what they believe and why. Push beyond the pat answers to find out what's in their heart. Be ready to share your beliefs *after* they've shared.
- Book suggestions regarding understanding truth with kids: *The Case for Christ for Kids* written by Lee Strobel.

YOUR NEXT STEP: _____

_____

_____

Conversation Ten – Parenting

LifeSign #5: Parenting by Example

Following your Lead: How consistently are your kids following your EXAMPLE of trusting Christ in difficulties and decisions?

Conversation Starters

What do you think?
1. Start here: What's the toughest part of being a parent for you? What is depleting or frustrating?
2. In what ways are you a *good* example for your kids of trusting Christ in times of stress, difficulty?
3. Is there anything you'd like to *change*—an area where you're *not* being a good example?

Biblical Foundations

What does God say?
- "Therefore, my beloved brethren, be steadfast, immovable, always abounding in the work of the Lord, knowing that your toil is not in vain in the Lord." (1 Corinthians 15:58, NASB)
- "Let us not become weary in doing good, for at the proper time we will reap a harvest if we do not give up." (Galatians 6:9)
- "But as for you, continue in what you have learned and have become convinced of, because you know those from whom you learned it, and how from infancy you have known the holy Scriptures, which are able to make you wise for salvation through faith in Christ Jesus." (2 Timothy 3:14-15)

Ideas for Growth

Okay, so now what?
- Book suggestions: *Grace Based Parenting* by Tim Kimmel, *Parenting by the Book, Biblical Wisdom for Raising Your Child* by John Rosemond.
- You cannot give what you don't have. Are you running on empty? Are you getting "fed" by taking in scripture on a regular basis?

Your Next Step: _____
_____
_____

LIFESIGNS: HOW ARE YOU? REALLY.

LIFESIGN #6: PURSUING A LARGER PURPOSE

Life with Purpose: Does it seem your kids want to live for something GREATER than themselves (finding and following a passion, giving themselves fully to Jesus and to a greater cause)

CONVERSATION STARTERS

What do you think?
1. What is an "entitlement mentality?" Do your kids have it?
2. What if we handed your kids $1,000 in cash, what would they do? What choices would they make?
3. How can you help your kids expand their vision for their lives, a Life with Purpose beyond themselves?

BIBLICAL FOUNDATIONS

What does God say?
- "For whoever wants to save his life will lose it, but whoever loses his life for Me and for the gospel will save it. What good is it for a man to gain the whole world, yet forfeit his soul?" (Mark 8:35-36)
- "Since, then, you have been raised with Christ, set your hearts on things above, where Christ is seated at the right hand of God. Set your minds on things above, not on earthly things." (Colossians 3:1-2)

IDEAS FOR GROWTH

Okay, so now what?
- This book will inspire your kids to dream big: *Love Does: Discover a Secretly Incredible Life in an Ordinary World* by Bob Goff. It is excellent!
- Have your teen or pre-teen read the book *Do Hard Things: A Teenage Rebellion Against Low Expectations* by Alex and Brett Harris. It will radically expand their thinking about living for a larger purpose.
- For perspective on living for something greater than yourself read *Death by Suburb* by Dave Goetz.

YOUR NEXT STEP: _____
_____
_____

Conversation Ten – Parenting

LifeSign #7: Influencing your Kids
Who, or what, INFLUENCES your children the most?

Conversation Starters

What do you think?
1. First, what's the difference between *influence* and *authority*?
2. Let's just answer the question: Who, or what, influences your kids the MOST? Friends? Social media? Music? Movies? Youth group?
3. Where do you, as the parent, fit on the list of influences in your kid(s) lives?

Biblical Foundations

What does God say?
- "See to it that no one takes you [or your kids] captive through hollow and deceptive philosophy, which depends on human tradition and the basic principles of this world, rather than on Christ." (Colossians 2:8)
- "These commandments that I give you today are to be upon your hearts. Impress them on your children. Talk about them when you sit at home and when you walk along the road, when you lie down and when you get up." (Deuteronomy 6:6-7)

Ideas for Growth

Okay, so now what?
- Ask yourself: How do my children spend their free time? Who do they hang out with? What media do they consume when you're not looking?
- Talk with your kids about the perils of social media.
- Read *Love is a Choice* by Hemfelt, Minirth & Meier.
- Media is a powerful influence on our children. Consider utilizing some kind of accountability software on phones and computers. Head over to www.InternetSafety.com for one of those resources.

Your Next Step: _____
_____
_____

Conversation Eleven

Freedom from Hurtful Habits

"The more you hurt, the more you'll hide"

These four men have become my best friends. We're close, like brothers.

The big guy on my right is a heroin addict. His arms are covered with tattoos and his knuckles are covered with scars. Without a word, they tell a story of chaos and violence. On my left is a sex addict. He's facing 8-16 years for doing something with a minor that makes me shudder. Next to him sits a good Christian friend; we often pray together. His methamphetamine habit and gambling addiction have cost him nearly everything.

Then there's my roommate. He's an alcoholic with post-traumatic stress disorder (PTSD). He did three tours in Iraq, most

Conversation Eleven – Hurtful Habits

of it in Baghdad, as an Army combat medic. Sometimes, in the middle of the night, he wakes up screaming.

I've always wondered what kind of people go to rehab—now I know. Wounded people. Lost people. Broken people.

People like me.

Honestly, I thought I'd be there for three weeks – I ended up staying for three months. How did a successful entrepreneur and author end up here, with these people? The wine I drank while hiding in my bedroom at night was only a symptom of a deeper problem. You see, I too was wounded, lost, and broken—just like the men in that room, men that I'd come to know and love.

This chapter is not about my story. It's about Jesus and your story. If you've ever felt stuck, trapped, or defeated by a hurtful habit, there is hope. You too can find freedom, and it's closer than you think.

Where do we start?

I'm not going to overwhelm you with statistics from the Centers for Disease Control (CDC) on addiction in America. For one thing, they're depressing. Plus, you'd rightly point out, "I'm not sure those stats apply to church-going Christians." Well guess what? We now have LifeSigns data on addictions—most of which comes from people who go to church.

A full eight years after creating LifeSigns, I finally felt ready to write a module on addictions, only we call them "Hurtful Habits," so we don't scare people away. This is an opt-in module, meaning you must deliberately choose to include it in your LifeSigns. We ask, *"Are you feeling controlled or trapped by a hurtful habit or compulsive behavior?"* Honestly, I had no idea how many people would choose to opt-in. Would it be 5%, 10%, or even 15% of our church-going population? In the end, the results were eye-opening.

LIFESIGNS: HOW ARE YOU? REALLY.

No less than 34% of those taking LifeSigns chose to include the Hurtful Habits module. *That's one in three people* who clicked the option that said, "Yes, I'm feeling controlled or trapped, and I want to talk about it." Even when we look at pastors and elders, the percentage of those struggling is the same. And I suspect many more people skipped it, when they should have clicked it. Another 8% of LifeSigns participants said, "I have a friend or loved-one who is trapped." So, if you're wrestling with a persistent struggle, you're not alone.

Now let's peek inside the responses to the Hurtful Habits module itself—only the numbers. We gently asked people: "What negative behaviors have you feeling stuck, trapped, or defeated?" It turns out, many people listed more than one issue.

Here's the breakdown:
- 44% – food issues: eating for comfort, binging, excessive junk food or sugar or caffeine, body image issues, eating disorders, excessive or compulsive dieting
- 41% – purity issues: pornography, lust, masturbation, sexting, fantasy, hooking-up using dating sites, etc.
- 23% – substance issues: alcohol, illegal drugs, prescription abuse, nicotine, etc.
- 10% – sex outside marriage (72% of which are female, 30% are married)
- 7% – escapism: isolating through excessive social media or television
- 5% – compulsive shopping, excessive spending
- 13% – other struggles (depression, anxiety, anger, laziness, shame, hoarding, etc.)

I'm not going to speculate on why food and porn, rather than drugs or alcohol, top the list of hurtful habits among church-going Christians. I can tell you that 75% of this population engages in these destructive behaviors daily, several times a week, or weekly. These are frequent, persistent struggles. If you're a Christian, wrestling with an addiction can shake the very foundations of your faith. It makes you wonder, "Why does Jesus seem to work for everyone else . . . but not for me?"

Yes, we're going to talk about how Christ sets you free. But first, it's vitally important to understand how you got trapped in the first place. This will actually be encouraging. Stay with me.

THE REAL PROBLEM: GOD SUBSTITUTES

Let's start with the Bible. The apostle John had outlived all the other apostles, his final years in Roman exile on the Greek island of Patmos. In the last verse, in one of his last letters, John issues a passionate plea: "Dear children, keep away from anything that might take God's place in your hearts" (1 John 5:21). Another version says, "Keep yourself from idols."

Let me translate: An idol is a God substitute. It's anything, other than Jesus, that you turn to for comfort or relief. Whether it's drugs, alcohol, food, gambling, or porn, they're all just God substitutes. That's why they take control—they take the place of God.

Paul put it clearly, "It is for freedom that Christ has set us free. Stand firm, then, and do not let yourselves be burdened again by a yoke of slavery" (Galatians 5:1). Addiction is slavery. Scripture says, "You are slaves of the one you obey" (Romans 6:16). Here's how it happens, one step at a time.

STEPS TO SLAVERY #1 – WE HIDE IT.

A decade ago, after 22 years of strife and struggle, my wife left me for someone else. Lying alone in that big bed, in that big house, the awful truth hit me like a sledgehammer: "She doesn't want me. And she's not coming back." Night after night a flood of memories—the good, the bad, and the ugly— battered my weary mind. Sleep was impossible. And I started drinking wine at night, in secret, with the door closed, away from my children. I'd taken the first step towards slavery: *I hid it.*

The LifeSigns data on Hurtful Habits tells a similar story. The majority of people indicate that, "I hide my struggle from family, friends, or co-workers." Only 6% have shared their struggle with a pastor or counselor.

Hiding is nothing new. The moment Adam and Eve ate the forbidden fruit in the garden, we're told "they suddenly felt shame at their nakedness. So they sewed fig leaves together to cover themselves" (Genesis 3:7). Sin may taste sweet, for a moment, but it quickly turns to bitter shame. When Adam and Eve "suddenly felt shame," *they hid from each other first*—even before they hid from God.

You've been there. You know how this works. The more you hurt, the more you hide. Over the years, I've turned to a truth in Proverbs that is both sobering and encouraging: "People who conceal (hide) their sins will not prosper," now here's the encouraging part, "but if they confess and turn from them, they will find compassion" (Proverbs 28:13). Did you catch that? When you choose to reveal and reject your God substitutes, you will find compassion—not condemnation.

So, may I ask a personal question? What are you hiding?

STEPS TO SLAVERY #2 – WE'RE ISOLATED BY IT.

I didn't announce my growing struggles with depression and alcohol to the world on social media. Quite the opposite, I began to wear a carefully constructed mask. But pretending became exhausting. Slowly, I withdrew from friends and family, feeling more and more like "The Invisible Man."

I'd taken the second step into slavery: *I was isolated by it.*

Addiction always leads to isolation. And isolation feeds addiction. It's a vicious cycle. The latest data we've collected from people struggling with a hurtful habit vividly illustrates the

Conversation Eleven – Hurtful Habits

addiction/isolation cycle. The lowest-scored LifeSigns items ever recorded are these two:

- Only 27% of the time: People reach out for help when they struggle with a hurtful habit (i.e., to a friend, counselor, support group, or pastor).
- Only 25% of the time: People try to be accountable to a friend or sponsor (i.e., staying in regular contact, being honest about progress or lack of progress).

For context, people who do not struggle with a hurtful habit are twice as likely to "maintain a healthy level of accountability" (55% of the time). Most people who struggle also checked the box that said, "I feel isolated or hopeless in my struggle." And like Adam and Eve, our data also shows that when you hide from people, you're more likely to hide from God.

Think back over the last few months. Are you becoming more connected, or more isolated?

Steps to Slavery #3 – We're defeated by it.

I valiantly tried to stop the slide. I went to 12-step meetings and got a sponsor. I did a searching and fearless moral inventory and made amends to people I'd wronged. I read and journaled and prayed. I visited addicts in the hospital on Christmas eve and made coffee at meetings. I was told to "trust the process." But inside, I felt like a raw, bloody mess. I still loved my (ex)wife. I couldn't let her go. I was tortured by thoughts of, "If only I could have, would have, should have," and by images of her in the arms of another man. Soon I turned back to alcohol to numb the pain.

I was utterly defeated. Slavery had become my reality.

The majority of people grappling with a hurtful habit, 59% to be exact, said "I tell myself, 'Never again!' only to do it again." And

49% said, "I notice it has gotten worse in the last month," and "I find I can't stop thinking about it." In other words, they feel defeated by it too.

You'd never think someone as spiritual and strong as the apostle Paul, someone who stood up to beatings and bullies, could feel defeated by sin. He did. In the book of Romans, we learn of his struggle. Paul wrote, "For what I am doing, I do not understand; for I am not practicing what I would like to do, but I am doing the very thing I hate" (Romans 7:15).

Can you relate to "doing the very thing I hate?" Me too.

This isn't the place to unearth the treasure trove of truth buried in Romans chapters 6-8. For that, you'll find a number of excellent resources at the back of this chapter. Let's jump to the end of Paul's story. He concludes, "I find then the principle that evil is present in me, the one who wants to do good. Wretched man that I am! Who will set me free from the body of this death? Thanks be to God through Jesus Christ our Lord!" (Romans 7:21-25).

Here's the point: Paul said, "Who will set me free," not "what." He trusted a person, not a process. Are the 12 Steps helpful? Yes, of course. Use them. But remember that true freedom from slavery comes through a person, Jesus Christ.

STEPS TO SLAVERY #4 – WE'RE DEFINED BY IT.

While I loved going to 12-step meetings, I hated the introductions. "Hi, my name is Scott and I'm an Alcoholic." Day after day, week after week, it was drilled into my brain, "This is who I am. This is who I'll always be: Alcoholic." I understand why they make us do it that way. It's a reminder and a warning. But here's the thing: It's not what is *most true* about me.

Here's the Truth: Your addiction is NOT your identity.

Conversation Eleven – Hurtful Habits

If you're a believer in Christ, a hurtful habit is not what is most true about you either. It took years of reminders from my pastor, Pete Briscoe, for this to sink in: My identity is not defined by my behavior—but by my Savior. That changes everything!

According to the LifeSigns data, most people with a hurtful habit say, "I sometimes wonder if God is disappointed or angry with me." Others feel, "If I'm enslaved, then I must not be saved." Those are lies from the pit of hell. Here's the truth:

- *You are New:* "If anyone is in Christ, the new creation has come: The old has gone, the new is here!"
  (2 Corinthians 5:17)
- *You are Clean:* "He chose us in him before the creation of the world to be holy and blameless in his sight."
  (Ephesians 1:4)
- *You are Accepted:* "You stand before Him without a single fault." (Colossians 1:22)

When you trust Jesus as Savior, you are fundamentally and forever changed. That voice in your head condemning you is NOT Jesus, and it is dangerous. Why? Because what you believe drives how you behave. Don't listen to the lies. You have a new identity, even if you can't see it or feel it—yet.

Let me summarize how the steps to slavery work: When we turn to a God substitute, we hide it. When we hide it, we become isolated by it. The more we're isolated, the more we're defeated by it. And when we feel defeated, it's easy to be defined by it.

May I ask: If you're feeling trapped or stuck, where are you on the steps to slavery? Hiding > Isolated > Defeated > Defined?

There is another path—one that leads to Life.

The Path to Finding Freedom: Step by Step

Are you hurting and hiding? Has your struggle defeated and defined you? Then I have good news: God has provided a way out. Jesus said it best, "The thief comes only to steal and kill and destroy; I came that they may have life and have it abundantly" (John 10:10). Jesus did not come to judge or condemn you, but to rescue you.

Here's a picture of how you can find the freedom and new Life that Jesus has promised, one step at a time:

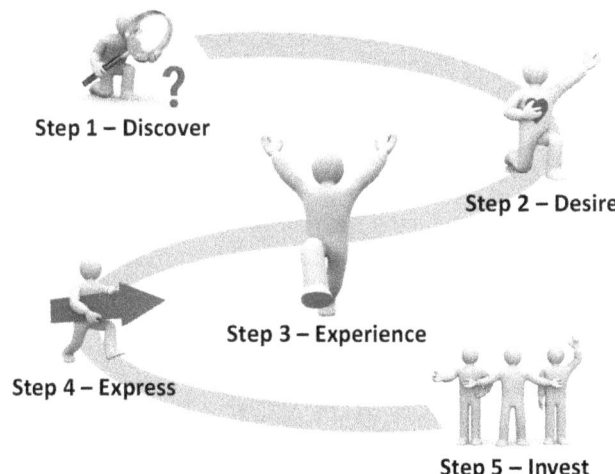

How does this work? First, this is not a self-help process. Each step to finding freedom is initiated by, empowered by, and guided by the Holy Spirit. That's why you'll see lots of scriptures as we explore each step below. Second, you can decide to follow Him on this journey or to stay stuck. You can choose to cooperate or to stagnate. You can respond or resist. It's up to you.

FINDING FREEDOM – STEP #1: WE DISCOVER IT.

Addictions don't develop overnight. A hurtful habit will slowly sneak up on you. Then, you wake up one morning and discover that you've lost control of your life. That realization is a good thing. Why? It is the first step from slavery to freedom.

Denial is willful blindness. It's hiding from yourself and from reality. That's why in LifeSigns, you asked God to "reveal any hurtful way in me" (Psalm 139:24). God might reveal a "hurtful way" by allowing you to suffer some painful consequences: a trip to the emergency room or jail, a lost job or lost marriage. The Spirit is using pain, not to punish, but to give you a new awareness of your situation. He also uses scripture to open your eyes: "For the word of God is alive and powerful...it exposes our innermost thoughts and desires" (Hebrews 4:12). Being "exposed" isn't much fun, but it is essential.

Second, the Spirit gives you a new awareness of God's provision. Paul prayed, "that the eyes of your heart may be enlightened in order that you may know the hope to which He has called you...and His incomparably great power for us who believe" (Ephesians 1:18-19). When you discover your true condition, as well as God's provision, you're poised to take the second step towards freedom.

FINDING FREEDOM – STEP #2: WE DESIRE IT.

Cravings are real. I was physically and emotionally dependent on alcohol—but never satisfied. A God substitute always leaves you feeling empty and wanting more. But no matter how numb you become; our gracious God provides moments of clarity. You'll hear Him whisper, "There is something better. Come away with Me. I will give you rest" (Matthew 11:28).

That's the second step on the road to freedom. The Spirit competes with your compulsions, planting the seeds of change in your heart. Scripture says, "God is working in you, giving you the *desire* and the *power* to do what pleases him" (Philippians 2:13). The Greek word for "working" is energéō, which literally means, "energizing." God provides two things you need to find freedom: the desire and the divine power to choose a different path.

There's a beautiful picture of how this process works, tucked away in the book of Acts: "A woman named Lydia, from the city of Thyatira, a seller of purple fabrics, a worshiper of God, was listening, and the Lord opened her heart to respond to the things spoken by Paul." (Acts 16:14).

Don't miss the progression: (1) Lydia turned to God, (2) she was listening, (3) the Lord opened her heart, and (4) she responded. Let's break it down: Lydia's job was to turn and listen. God's job was to change her heart and enable her to take action. Both you and God have a role in this.

Stop and listen. This could be a moment of clarity. What new desire is God whispering to your heart?

Finding Freedom – Step #3: We experience it.

I've experienced defeat, when recovery seems impossible. It's like I'm caught in a raging river, helpless and hopeless, flailing and gasping for breath as I'm dragged to the depths. I've also experienced victory, when recovery is easy. It's a totally different experience. I'm carried along by a deep current, floating in my innertube, effortlessly propelled towards freedom on the smooth river of God's grace.

But let's be honest, most days are a mixture of both. I've experienced victory and defeat, sometimes within the span of a single hour. What's the difference? It's where I'm looking to find Life. The Bible says there are only two options: "Whoever has the Son has life; whoever does not have God's Son does not have life" (1 John 5:12). I'll let Jesus explain from John 4.

One hot afternoon in Palestine, weary and thirsty from a long journey, Jesus did something scandalous. He struck up a conversation with a female sex addict sitting by a well. She was shocked, and said "Why are you talking to me?" Jesus replied, "If you only knew the gift God has for you and who you are speaking to, you would ask me, and I would give you living water."

She was intrigued, "God has gift for me? Living water?" She was also confused, "But sir, where would you get this living water? And besides, do you think you're greater than our ancestor Jacob, who gave us this well? How can you offer better water than he and his sons and his animals enjoyed?"

Conversation Eleven – Hurtful Habits

Jesus offered her better water—living water.

He replied, "Anyone who drinks this water will soon become thirsty again. But those who drink the water I give will never be thirsty again. It becomes a fresh, bubbling spring within them, giving them eternal life." Jesus offered her a *new source of Life.* How did she respond? "Please, sir," the woman said, "give me this water! Then I'll never be thirsty again" (John 4:6-15).

Jesus knew everything about her God substitutes—and her thirst. Even with five sexual partners, she remained parched, empty, and unfulfilled. Only Jesus can quench your thirst. Only He is the source of Life. The more you "taste and see that the Lord is good," the more you will find freedom and experience new Life.

Which begs the question: What, and more importantly, who are you turning to for Life?

Finding Freedom – Step #4: We express it.

Recovery takes time. When I learned how to trust Jesus as my source of strength, He began to put my shattered world back together. My house got cleaner and my finances got better. My depression lifted and my health improved. The chains of isolation were broken, and my relationships were restored. My kids got their dad back. My parents got their son back. God slowly changed my life, from the inside out.

Jesus said, "My Father who *lives in me* does his work *through me*" (John 14:10). The same is true for you.

At its core, finding freedom is incredibly simple: You're learning to allow Jesus to live *in you*, so that Jesus can live *through you*. He used an analogy to explain how this works. Jesus said, "I am the vine; you are the branches. If you remain in me and I in you, you will bear much fruit; apart from me you can do nothing" (John 15:5). That makes sense. The more you stay connected to Christ (the vine), the more new growth you'll experience (the fruit). You're not in this alone.

LifeSigns: How are you? Really.

Here's the problem: I'm flakey. Even though Jesus will "never leave me or forsake me," I don't always "remain" or "abide" in Christ. I get discouraged and distracted. I slip back into isolation. That's why relationships with other people are essential to finding freedom and keeping it.

Addiction feeds on isolation. So even now, years into my recovery, I do two things every day to combat isolation. I schedule time with people—it doesn't matter who. Second, every day I ask someone for help—it doesn't matter for what. Why are these still a part of my daily routine? Because, I've learned that hiding and pretending can kill me.

When Paul was coaching a young leader, he used the same strategy. He told Timothy, "Pursue righteousness, faith, love and peace, *with those* who call on the Lord from a pure heart" (2 Timothy 2:22). Your chances of finding freedom drastically improve when you pursue it with people who are also looking to Jesus for Life.

As you walk the road to recovery, WHO is with you?

Finding Freedom – Step #5: We invest it.

I have a confession. When I was asked to start a little recovery ministry at my church, the number one reason I said "Yes" wasn't because I wanted to help others—though I did. It wasn't because I wanted to share what I'd learned—thought I'd learned where to find Life. I said "Yes" primarily because it would help me to stay free too.

Want to supercharge your recovery? Help other people find freedom. Believe it or not, your wounds and weakness, your fears and failures, those are not liabilities—they're some of your greatest assets. You can invest them in three ways: comforting others, motivating others, and equipping others. When you do, it's like high-octane jet fuel. You'll go further and faster than ever before. It will help you stay free.

Conversation Eleven – Hurtful Habits

First, you're uniquely equipped to comfort others because, "God comforts us in all our troubles so that we can comfort others." (2 Corinthians 1:4). Second, your story will motivate others to find freedom as you, "think of ways to motivate one another to acts of love and good works" (Hebrews 10:24). Third, you can equip others as you, "teach these truths to other trustworthy people who will be able to pass them on to others." (2 Tim 2:2).

Jesus said it best, "Freely you received, freely give" (Matthew 10:8). Freedom in Christ is a gift you keep—by giving it away.

So, are you trusting Jesus and sober today? Good. Invest in someone who isn't. You'll both reap the rewards.

The Bottom Line: You can be free.

I love our little recovery support group at my church. Every week, people find freedom precisely to the degree that they "don't let anything take God's place in your heart" (1 John 5:21). We help people understand that an addiction is ultimately a *worship disorder*. Change what you worship, it changes *who* and *what* is in charge of your life.

We've covered a lot of ground, and you may feel a bit overwhelmed. That's okay. The steps to finding freedom are pretty simple:

- Step #1 – Discover: as God opens your eyes, you discover you've lost your freedom
- Step #2 – Desire: as you discover what's missing, God gives you the desire for a new life
- Step #3 – Experience: as God changes your heart, you make better choices and experience true freedom
- Step #4 – Express: as you experience life internally, you begin to express it externally
- Step #5 – Invest: as you learn to live differently, God enables you to invest in others who need to be set free

Walking the steps to freedom is not a one-and-done occurrence. It's a daily decision to move from *hurtful* habits to *helpful* habits—like turning to Jesus as your source of strength, hope, and power. It's a cycle of renewal where you get a "do-over" anytime you need it. And if you're not sure about your role and God's role in this process, then pray as David prayed, "Show me the right path, O Lord; point out the road for me to follow" (Psalm 25:4). You'll soon discover that each step to finding freedom is guided by a Savior who is always looking for wounded people, lost people, and broken people.

People like you and me.

Jesus is waiting for you to stop running away. Turn around and run into his arms.

He will set you free.

> *"Let anyone who is thirsty come.
> Let anyone who desires
> drink freely from the water of life."*
> – Revelation 22:17

> *"He has sent me to comfort the brokenhearted
> and to proclaim that captives will be released
> and prisoners will be freed."*
> – Isaiah 61:1

Conversation Eleven – Hurtful Habits

LifeSign #1: Grasping God's Grace

Unconditional Love: When you struggle, remembering that God loves you and cares for you — no matter what (trusting in God's grace, not your performance)

CONVERSATION STARTERS

What do you think?
1. When you blow it, what goes through your mind? What does "that voice" in your head say about you?
2. When you listen to those lies, how do you feel? How do those lies affect the way you see yourself?
3. Let's get practical: How can you recognize and replace lies with the truth? (i.e., Many times I've called my sister, shared the lies, and she speaks the Truth back to me. Then prays with me.)

BIBLICAL FOUNDATIONS

What does God say?
- "But because of His great love for us, God, who is rich in mercy, made us alive with Christ even when we were dead in transgressions—it is by grace you have been saved." Ephesians 2:4-6
- "Therefore, there is now no condemnation for those who are in Christ Jesus, because through Christ Jesus the law of the Spirit who gives life has set you free from the law of sin and death." Romans 8:1-2

IDEAS FOR GROWTH

Okay, so now what?
- If you're feeling condemned for your struggles, that voice is *not* Jesus. It's a lie. Write the two verses above on index cards and carry them with you. Truth is a powerful antidote to lies and shame.
- Check out *God's Astounding Opinion of You* by Ralph Harris. And this short read has helped many people: *Seeing Yourself Through God's Eyes* by June Hunt.

Your Next Step: _____
_____
_____

LifeSigns: How are you? Really.

LifeSign #2: Rigorous Honesty

Honesty: Being honest with yourself about how your habit is HURTING yourself and others (not in denial, seeing the impact, taking ownership)

CONVERSATION STARTERS

What do you think?
1. How do we tend to *minimize* a hurtful habit? (i.e., I'm not as bad as _____.)
2. In what ways do we *justify* our negative behaviors? (i.e., Just one more time, I've had an awful day.)
3. How has your hurtful habit negatively affected other people? Be specific. (i.e., I missed my daughter's game because I was at home sleeping it off.)

BIBLICAL FOUNDATIONS

What does God say?
- "He who conceals his transgressions will not prosper, but he who confesses and forsakes them will find compassion." Proverbs 28:13
- "But speaking the truth in love, we are to grow up in all aspects into Him who is the head, even Christ... Therefore, laying aside falsehood, speak truth each one of you with his neighbor, for we are members of one another." Ephesians 4:15, 25

IDEAS FOR GROWTH

Okay, so now what?
- You may use a journal, but it's a powerful tool. You don't have to share this: Write out your hurtful habit, then list all ways it negatively impacts you—and people around you. Painful, but very helpful.
- Check out the book *Redemption* by Mike Wilkerson for help on how to stop hiding and start trusting Jesus for your recovery from hurtful habits.
- Memorize Psalm 119:11, "I have hidden your word in my heart that I may not sin against you."

YOUR NEXT STEP: _____
_____
_____

Conversation Eleven – Hurtful Habits

LifeSign #3: Freedom in Christ

Faith in Action: On a daily basis, putting your TRUST in Jesus— knowing that He can change your heart, character, and behavior (leaning on Christ as your source of strength, life, and peace)

Conversation Starters

What do you think?
1. Start here: What specific issue in your life have you tried to change, and it has *not* improved?
2. Do you really believe that Jesus can change you? Or does that only apply to more "spiritual" people?
3. What did Jesus mean when He said, "With man this is impossible, but not with God; all things are possible with God"? (Mark 10:27) Does that really apply to your hurtful habits?

Biblical Foundations

What does God say?
- "I can do everything through Christ, who gives me strength." (Philippians 4:13)
- "So, if you think you are standing firm, be careful that you don't fall! No temptation has seized you except what is common to man. And God is faithful; he will not let you be tempted beyond what you can bear. But when you are tempted, he will also provide a way out so that you can stand up under it." (1 Corinthians 10:12-13), For context read the whole chapter of 1 Corinthians 10.

Ideas for Growth

Okay, so now what?
- Need someone to pray with you? Reach out to your local church and ask to speak to someone in their care and support ministry (pastor, counselor).
- See *God's Astounding Opinion of You* by Ralph Harris. Also, this has helped many people: *Seeing Yourself Through God's Eyes* by June Hunt.

Your Next Step: _____
_____
_____

LifeSigns: How are you? Really.

LifeSign #4: Avoiding Isolation

Getting Help: Are you REACHING OUT for help when you struggle? (to a friend, counselor, support group, or pastor)

Conversation Starters

What do you think?
1. Why is it so hard to ask for help, especially for a hurtful habit?
2. How does guilt or shame keep us isolated in our struggles?
3. Who can you turn to that could provide support and encouragement? Be specific.

What does God say?

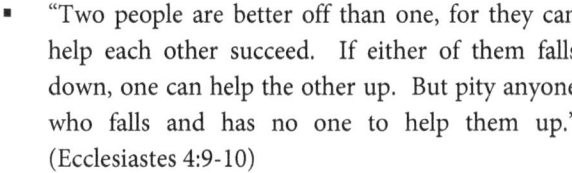
Biblical Foundations

- "Two people are better off than one, for they can help each other succeed. If either of them falls down, one can help the other up. But pity anyone who falls and has no one to help them up." (Ecclesiastes 4:9-10)
- "Do not merely listen to the word, and so deceive yourselves. Do what it says. Whoever looks intently into the perfect law that gives freedom, and continues in it—not forgetting what they have heard, but doing it—they will be blessed in what they do." (James 1:22-25)

Ideas for Growth

Okay, so now what?
- You're allowed to have a "support team." It could include a friend, counselor, pastor, doctor, and even a recovery group. You don't have to go it alone!
- Pick up a copy of *Sidetracked in the Wilderness* by Michael Wells to learn about trusting God and asking others for help.

Your Next Step: _____
_____
_____

Conversation Eleven – Hurtful Habits

LifeSign #5: Healthy Accountability

Healthy Accountability: Staying ACCOUNTABLE to a friend or sponsor (staying in regular contact, being honest about your progress or lack of progress)

Conversation Starters

What do you think?
1. When we talk about accountability, WHO are you being accountable to? Here's a hint: "So then, each of us will give an account of ourselves to God." (Romans 14:12)
2. Who can you link arms with that is open to sharing some mutual encouragement on a weekly basis?

Biblical Foundations

What does God say?
- "Therefore confess your sins to each other and pray for each other so that you may be healed. The prayer of a righteous person is powerful and effective." (James 5:16)
- "Above all else, guard your heart, for it is the wellspring of life." (Proverbs 4:23)
- "Listen, my sons, to a father's instruction; pay attention and gain understanding. I give you sound learning, so do not forsake my teaching." (Proverbs 4:1-2)

Ideas for Growth

Okay, so now what?
- Identify someone you can invite to coffee and ask to share accountability and encouragement on a weekly basis.
- Pick up a copy of *Sidetracked in the Wilderness* by Michael Wells to learn about trusting God and asking others for help.

Your Next Step: _____
_____
_____

LifeSigns: How are you? Really.

LifeSign #6: Your True Identity

Identity: Recognizing that your behavior is NOT your identity, but that your TRUE IDENTITY is in Christ alone (as a Christian you are God's adopted child, a new creation, redeemed, renewed, covered by grace)

Conversation Starters

What do you think?
1. When you introduce yourself to someone new, in addition to your name, how do you describe yourself? ("I'm an engineer" "I'm a Cowboys fan")
2. Paul said in Romans 12:2, "Be transformed by the renewing of your mind." How does a change in your thinking result in a change in your behavior?

Biblical Foundations

What does God say?
- "I have been crucified with Christ and I no longer live, but Christ lives in me. The life I now live in the body, I live by faith in the Son of God, who loved me and gave himself for me." (Galatians 2:20)
- "I pray that the eyes of your heart may be enlightened in order that you may know the hope to which he has called you, the riches of his glorious inheritance in his holy people, and his incomparably great power for us who believe." (Ephesians 1:18-19)

Ideas for Growth

Okay, so now what?
- Going to recovery support meetings is a great way to "renew your mind." That's why you'll leave feeling better than when you got there.
- Check out *God's Astounding Opinion of You* by Ralph Harris. This short read has helped many people embrace their true identity: *Seeing yourself through God's Eyes* by June Hunt.

Your Next Step: _____
_____
_____

Conversation Twelve

Single Life

"I have learned the secret of being content in any and every situation."
– Paul, a single person, in Philippians 4:12

L et's get right to the heart of the biggest challenge in single life: *being alone.*

We took a deep dive into the LifeSigns data from thousands of single people, in all the ages and stages of life, and uncovered some surprising insights. While there are dozens of ingredients that contribute to living a happy, healthy, and fulfilling single life, in our analysis, we pinpointed several key differences among people who are experiencing God's best as a single.

Conversation Twelve – Single Life

First, where do most single people want to see change? According to the latest LifeSigns results, the #1 growth priority people selected, by a two-to-one margin, was this:

"Loneliness: When you feel intense emotional or physical LONGING for another person, finding PEACE in Jesus (when the desire for romance or sex seems overwhelming, turning to Christ for comfort)"

Not only is dealing with loneliness the highest growth priority, it also happens to be the lowest scored (least healthy) area we covered in the Single Life section. So, what's *different* about people who are not struggling with loneliness? The answers may surprise you.

Looking for Love—In All the Right Places

We compared people who are *more lonely* with those who are *less lonely* to determine what's different. Would less lonely people belong to a healthy small group? Yes. Would less lonely people pursue their passions and serve in ministry? Yes. Connecting with others and serving play a significant role in experiencing less loneliness. But the single biggest difference among singles who were less lonely was this: sexual purity.

The link between sexual purity and loneliness seems counterintuitive, meaning, it's the *opposite* of what we'd expect. It's easy to assume that sexual activity (whether on-line or in-person) will satisfy our desires for intimacy and companionship.

It does not.

Here's the reality: Singles who are *more sexually active*, whether on-line or in-person, are *more lonely*. Said differently, seeking sexual intimacy outside of marriage does not satisfy—it does exactly the opposite—it leaves us feeling empty, unfulfilled, and lonely (see graph).

The LINK between Loneliness and Sexual Purity

Are you sexually PURE in thoughts and actions?

- Almost Never: 38%
- Rarely: 45%
- Sometimes: 61%
- Frequently: 79%
- Almost Always: 85%

Loneliness: Do you find peace and comfort in Christ?

Look at the graph from left to right. On the left are people who "almost never" or "rarely" find peace and comfort in Christ when they're feeling lonely. The vertical bars indicate how often they are staying "sexually pure in thought and action," on a scale of 0-100% of the time. Follow the graph towards the right and we can a positive correlation: The *more* sexually pure we are, the *less* lonely we feel. Purity = Peace.

Intimacy with Christ

The second most significant factor we found that contributes to experiencing *less loneliness* was this:

> *"Intimacy with Christ: On any given day, having an INTIMATE encounter with Jesus (being fully aware of His presence, hearing His voice, experiencing His peace)*

We shouldn't be surprised. David, who had his own issues with sexual purity, understood where to look for true satisfaction: "Whom have I in heaven but You? I desire You more than anything on earth. As for me, the nearness of God is my good" (Psalm 73:25, 28).

Conversation Twelve – Single Life

Bottom Line: Singles who pursue sexual purity and intimacy with Christ are less lonely, more content, and have more confidence and security for their future.

So, as you prepare to dive into the discussion questions that follow, please pay special attention to the LINK between your level of daily intimacy with Christ and your overall health and happiness as a single.

And remember what the apostle Paul, living and working as a single person, wrote to the believers in Philippi: "My God will supply all your needs according to His riches in glory in Christ Jesus" (Philippians 4:19).

Where are you seeking satisfaction?

Where are you "looking for love?"

Could it be that you're not as single as you think you are?

LifeSigns: How are you? Really.

LifeSign #1: Contentment in Single Life

Contentment: Learning to be truly CONTENT in single life (not waiting to experience and enjoy a full life until you get married, content in your current situation)

Conversation Starters

What do you think?
1. What negative perceptions do people sometimes have about people who are not married?
2. What don't you like about single life?
3. On the flip side, what are the advantages?

Biblical Foundations

What does God say?
- "I am not saying this because I am in need, for I have learned to be content whatever the circumstances. I know what it is to be in need, and I know what it is to have plenty. I have learned the secret of being content in any and every situation, whether well fed or hungry, whether living in plenty or in want." (Philippians 4:11-12)
- "But godliness with contentment is great gain. For we brought nothing into the world, and we can take nothing out of it. But if we have food and clothing, we will be content with that." (1 Timothy 6:6-8)

Ideas for Growth

Okay, so now what?
- Read Gary Thomas' book, *Sacred Pathways*, and discover the unique wiring of your spiritual temperament. It will help you find connection with Christ and contentment in your life.
- Does fear you won't be married drive your dating choices or behavior? Have you surrendered your dating life to Jesus? Is He in charge or are you?
- Search the site called OnePlace.com for sermons and articles on dating and relationships.

Your Next Step: _____

_____

_____

Conversation Twelve – Single Life

LifeSign #2: Initiating Relationships

Friendships: How often do you INITIATE relationships with other people? (rather than withdrawing or waiting for someone else to take the initiative with you)

CONVERSATION STARTERS

What do you think?
1. What makes it difficult to make new friends?
2. Exactly HOW do you initiate a new relationship with someone—without it being awkward?
3. When you've try, how do people typically respond?

BIBLICAL FOUNDATIONS

What does God say?
- "Let us consider how we may spur one another on toward love and good deeds, not giving up meeting together, as some are in the habit of doing, but encouraging one another—and all the more as you see the Day approaching." (Hebrews 10:24-25)
- "If we walk in the light as He Himself is in the light, we have fellowship with one another, and the blood of Jesus cleanses us from all sin." (1 John 1:7)

IDEAS FOR GROWTH

Okay, so now what?
- Better Together: The most satisfying expression of biblical community can be found in "group life." People connected with a small group of friends who are mutually committed to caring for one another, grow in their faith and impact others for Christ. In other words, a small group is an ideal setting for friends to "do life together."
- How comfortable are you at making friends? How well are you truly known and cared for? Are you currently meeting regularly with a small group of friends? If not, would you prayerfully consider the option of joining a small group?

YOUR NEXT STEP: _____
_____
_____

LifeSigns: How are you? Really.

LifeSign #3: Trusting God with Your Future

Security: Putting your TRUST in God for your future (believing He will supply all your needs, guide your decisions about career, relationships, finances)

CONVERSATION STARTERS

What do you think?
1. Let's be honest: Do you really trust God? Do you really believe He will guide and care for you?
2. Why is it sometimes hard to trust God for your future? (marriage, career, family, finances, etc.)

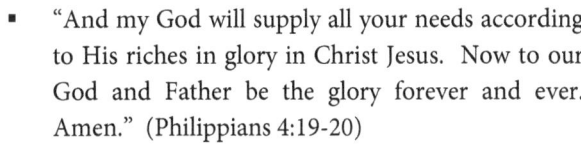

BIBLICAL FOUNDATIONS

What does God say?
- "And my God will supply all your needs according to His riches in glory in Christ Jesus. Now to our God and Father be the glory forever and ever. Amen." (Philippians 4:19-20)
- "Therefore I tell you, do not worry about your life, what you will eat or drink; or about your body, what you will wear. Is not life more than food, and the body more than clothes? Look at the birds of the air; they do not sow or reap or store away in barns, and yet your heavenly Father feeds them. Are you not much more valuable than they? Can any one of you by worrying add a single hour to your life?" (Matthew 6:25-27)

IDEAS FOR GROWTH

Okay, so now what?
- Debt takes a toll on us financially, emotionally, relationally, and spiritually. In less than two hours, the *Eliminating Debt* video study will help you create a plan to attack your debt and be free from the dangers of debt dependence (Crownonline.org).
- Check out one of the money-managing tools like Mint (www.mint.com) for your smartphone.

Your Next Step: _____
_____
_____

Conversation Twelve – Single Life

LifeSign #4: Serving Others

Serving: Engaging in SERVICE to others (using the gifts, talents and passions God has given you—plus the freedom that comes with being single)

Conversation Starters

What do you think?
1. Quick. What are your top three gifts? Don't worry about the terminology, what comes effortlessly?
2. Share one example of how you've allowed God to use your gifts to bless others. Anything goes.

What does God say?
- "I would like you to be free from concern. An unmarried man is concerned about the Lord's affairs—how he can please the Lord. But a married man is concerned about the affairs of this world—how he can please his wife—and his interests are divided." (1 Corinthians 7:32-34)
- "For we are God's handiwork, created in Christ Jesus to do good works, which God prepared in advance for us to do." (Ephesians 2:10)
- "For even the Son of Man did not come to be served, but to serve, and to give his life as a ransom for many." (Mark 10:45)

Biblical Foundations

Ideas for Growth

Okay, so now what?
- Don't know what spiritual gifts you have? Head over to spiritualgiftstest.com for a free gifts test for both adults and youth.
- Don't know your passions? Make a list of things that really "bother you" when you look at the world today. Pick up a copy of *Who Is My Neighbor?* by Steve Moore. It will help you to pinpoint your passions.

Your Next Step: _____
_____
_____

LifeSigns: How are you? Really.

LifeSign #5: Sexual Purity

Purity: Staying sexually PURE in thoughts and actions (living free from lust, pornography, or sex outside of marriage)

CONVERSATION STARTERS

What do you think?
1. What does our current society say about sexual purity? What's considered "acceptable?"
2. How does the internet, plus having a smart phone make it more difficult to pursue purity?
3. Should Christians "date?" If so, how do you date in a way that honors God?

BIBLICAL FOUNDATIONS

What does God say?
- "For you know what instructions we gave you by the authority of the Lord Jesus. It is God's will that you should be sanctified: that you should avoid sexual immorality; that each of you should learn to control your own body in a way that is holy and honorable, not in passionate lust like the pagans, who do not know God; and that in this matter no one should wrong or take advantage of a brother or sister. For God did not call us to be impure, but to live a holy life." (1 Thessalonians 4:1-8)

IDEAS FOR GROWTH

Okay, so now what?
- Dating is usually on the minds of single adults. Desiring a spouse is not wrong, but making that search your life's focus can be harmful, leading you to compromise your sexual purity. Evaluate your approach to dating: Are you pursuing relationships in a healthy way?
- Check out Elisabeth Elliot's classic book, *Passion and Purity: Learning to Bring Your Love Life Under Christ's Control*. It's both practical and encouraging.

YOUR NEXT STEP: _____
_____
_____

Conversation Twelve – Single Life

LifeSign #6: Loneliness

Loneliness: When you feel intense emotional or physical LONGING for another person, finding PEACE in your relationship with Jesus (when the desire for romance or sex seems overwhelming, turning to Christ for comfort)

Conversation Starters

What do you think?
1. Everyone experiences loneliness from time to time. When do you tend to feel the most lonely?
2. Can you share about a time when you found real comfort and peace in Christ—even as you were alone and wanted human companionship?

Biblical Foundations

What does God say?
- "And my God will supply all your needs according to His riches in glory in Christ Jesus. Now to our God and Father be the glory forever and ever. Amen." (Philippians 4:19-20)
- "Let us then approach God's throne of grace with confidence, so that we may receive mercy and find grace to help us in our time of need." (Hebrews 4:16)
- "But grow in grace, and in the knowledge of our Lord and Savior Jesus Christ." (2 Peter 3:18)

Ideas for Growth

Okay, so now what?
- Select a friend whom you trust and share your challenges with loneliness, pray together, hold each other accountable to lean into your relationship with Christ.
- Cru.org is loaded with practical ideas and insights on dating and relationships. Go to Train & Grow > Life & Relationships to explore.

Your Next Step: _____
_____
_____

The Last Chapter

Taking a Step of Faith

"...and lead me in the everlasting way."
– Psalm 139:24b

Okay, so now what?

Let's go back to the beginning of your LifeSigns journey. You've walked in the magnificent footsteps of David, a man after God's own heart, by praying as David prayed from Psalm 139, "Search me, O God…" Your vertical conversation has opened the door for the Spirit to speak freely to the deepest issues in your life. And your horizontal conversation freed you from isolation, offered encouragement, and provided you with some healthy accountability. These are critical conversations that can change your life.

While your two LifeSigns conversations are a powerful catalyst for growth, they are only the beginning. Now you may be wondering, "How do I turn my good intentions into actions?" The purpose of this last chapter is to explore some Biblical principles for taking a step of faith, even when you're fearful, doubtful, or have tried before and failed.

Finding and Following God's Will

Like Maurice Ravel's famous piece, Boléro, Psalm 139 is a 15-minute crescendo, leading to a dramatic climax. It is a grand invitation to dance. In this beloved Psalm, after a lifetime of candid conversations with God—from tears in a dark cave to shouts of victory atop the throne of Israel—David reveals just how deeply we are known by God. Psalm 139 vividly describes a heavenly Father who "understands your thoughts from afar" and "is intimately acquainted with all your ways. Even before there is a word on my tongue, Behold, O Lord, You know it all" (v. 3-4).

But Psalm 139 describes more than God's omniscience (all knowing), it also describes the depth of God's affection for you. God isn't just collecting data on your life, like some super-computer in the sky, recording your every thought and move. God is in love with you! You capture His full attention. He's not distant or distracted, but rather, you fill His thoughts day and night. As David writes, "How precious also are Your thoughts to me, O God! How vast is the sum of them! If I should count them, they would outnumber the sand" (v. 17-18). Every time I go to the beach, I marvel at how many grains of sand fit in the palm of my hand. I marvel that God loves me so much.

With God's tender love and His full knowledge of the smallest details of your life firmly in mind, let's look again at the last two verses of Psalm 139, with fresh eyes.

> *"Search me, O God, and know my heart;*
> *Try me and know my anxious thoughts;*
> *And see if there be any hurtful way in me,*
> *And lead me in the everlasting way."* - Psalm 139:23-24

One of the best ways to discover how scripture applies to your life is to pinpoint the *verbs*. The *verbs* always point to the action, and to who is taking the action. So carefully note the first four verbs in this text. You've asked God to *search you*, to *try you*, to *know you*, and to *see you*. In this case, God is the one doing the diagnosis. Not you.

Now, let's zero-in on that last, critical verb in Psalm 139: "And *lead* me in the everlasting way." The original Hebrew word for lead, *nachah*, literally means to *guide* or to *straighten*. You're saying, in effect, "God, in light of everything you've revealed to me, the depths of my heart, the anxieties of my mind, and the hurtful ways I sometimes live—in light of your awesome love and affection for me—where do I go from here? I'm ready to follow You. Show me the way." (see below)

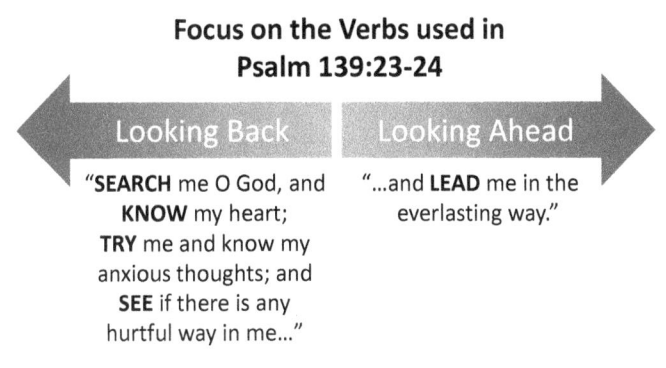

As the arrows suggest, with LifeSigns we're not just looking back by asking, "How are you?" We're also *looking forward* by asking, "What's your next step?" While there's tremendous value in your vertical and horizontal conversations, that's not the ultimate goal. As Jesus said to his first disciples, His voice still beckons you to "follow Me."

Here's the challenge. Following Jesus is, more often than not, a step into the unknown—it requires a step of faith. Getting a haircut or going to the grocery store doesn't require much faith. However, launching a new career, confronting an abusive co-

The Last Chapter: Step of Faith

worker, forgiving a wayward spouse, or sharing Christ with your neighbor—now those steps take faith!

So how do you step out in faith, rather than in the flesh? How do you move from where you are now, into the new life God has for you?

Living in "The Gap"

At the bottom of each section in LifeSigns, we simply asked: "Given all we've discussed, what step of faith, large or small, is God leading you to take when it comes to your _____?" (i.e., marriage, career, relationships, finances, kids, etc.).

For people who've spent time at church, the idea of "taking a step of faith" is old news. Don't dismiss this so quickly, just because you've heard it before. A step of faith may be common sense, but it's not common practice. We all live in the tension of what I call, "The Gap." It's the awkward distance between our beliefs and our behaviors, between hearing God's voice and our decision to follow.

Yes, the finished work of Christ on the cross provides you a brand-new identity. Yes, once you've placed your trust in Him, you're a "new creation," and you have the freedom to live victoriously (Colossians 2:13-15). But to be honest, too often my actions fall woefully short of my aspirations. Even when the Lord's leading is clear—and I hate to admit this—I'm dreadfully slow to respond. In some cases, I've plugged my ears and dragged my feet for weeks, or months, or years.

You already know that LifeSigns is not about self-evaluation. To be perfectly clear, *it's not about self-improvement either.* Any bookstore, gym, personal trainer, or financial planner can give you a self-improvement program. Those kinds of plans are both good and helpful, but taking a step of faith is radically different. How so? You're not just following ten rules to drop ten pounds—you're following Jesus into the mystery of a deeper relationship with Him. Taking a Spirit-led step of faith is about allowing Christ to work *in* you and *through* you. It's allowing Him to lead you into new places you'd never go on your own.

So, let's put the real issue squarely on the table. Do you ever wonder, *"How's it going to be different this time? Can I really change? Should I take the risk, and step out in faith?"* If you've ever tried to follow God's leading and fallen short, if you've ever felt that real change is impossible, then you're not alone. Even the apostle Paul wrestled with "The Gap" when he said, "I have the desire to do what is good, but I cannot carry it out" (Romans 7:18). A few verses later, Paul also describes the solution: "Do not walk according to the flesh but according to the Spirit" (Romans 8:4).

Here's the point: All those maddening gaps in your life—in your marriage, your finances, your career, your ministry—they all represent God-given opportunities to experience new life in Christ. But at the same time, deep lasting change can be difficult and discouraging. We make resolutions and we break them. We change for a season and then slip back into old habits. You may sometimes feel it's just not worth the effort, it's too painful, or that God has surely run out of patience. Relax. Your life and your growth are in His gentle hands.

So, whether you're motivated by aspirations (dreams) or by desperation (fears), let's see what the Bible says about closing the gap, and discovering God's grace along the way.

Step of Faith: Your Part, God's Part

Here's some good news: Paul proclaimed, "I am confident of this very thing, that He who began a good work in you will carry it on to completion until the day of Christ Jesus" (Philippians 1:6). The work that God began in you, He will also complete. You are His workmanship. Your personal growth is about His power and His plans, not yours. So first and foremost, remember that God is both the *author* and the *perfecter* of your faith (Hebrews 12:1-2).

Any step of faith has two key components: faith + action. First, by faith you're trusting God for direction, for His power, and for the ultimate outcome. That's what makes a step of faith fundamentally different from any human self-improvement program. Anything that causes you to stop, to consider the risks, and to squint into the swirling mists of uncertainty—requires a response in faith. And it's supposed to work that way. Because, "without faith it is impossible to please God, because anyone who comes to him must believe that he exists and that he rewards those who earnestly seek him" (Hebrews 11:6).

Second, taking a "step of faith" means you're going to get up and move! It's more than setting a new direction or adopting some new priorities—there's effort, exertion, and in some cases, copious amounts of perspiration involved. This is not a passive faith. It's an active, vigorous faith.

James strikes the balance between faith and action by asking: "What good is it, my brothers and sisters, if someone claims to have faith but has no deeds?…Faith by itself, if it is not accompanied by action, is dead" (James 2). Faith and action always go together, or they should.

Aspiration or Desperation: What Drives You?

A step of faith is initiated by, dependent on, and enabled by the Holy Spirit. I've found that God uses two conditions to grab my attention and move me to action: *aspiration* and *desperation.*

When God puts a dream in your heart, a vision for your future, or a burden for those missing the grace of God—that is aspiration at work. When the Spirit grabs your heart with a passion to make a difference in the lives of others, that is aspiration. Big goals and bold dreams usually come with big risks—they require faith. God-given aspirations, whether for your family, your career, your marriage, or your ministry can be powerful motivators.

Pain can also be a powerful motivator—that is *desperation* at work. A couple of years before I met my adopted big brother Billy, he was at the end of his rope. With his permission, I'll share part of a letter Billy sent me after reading the first edition of the LifeSigns book.

> When I took that "step of faith" to join Mercy Ships, it wasn't so much an act of obedience as it was desperation. Here I was cooking for one of the richest men in the world, known all over Austin and much of Texas for my charity work, and I was not far from death's door. I was an alcoholic and a drug addict. Not like I was breaking into people's houses to get money for crack, but I would take anything anyone put in front of me. I reached a realization that my time was running out. I had a "conversation" with God and told Him if something didn't drastically change, I would be dead in six months. My only prayer at that point was that I wouldn't take anyone else with me when it happened (i.e., drinking and driving). I was almost beaten to death by my "best friend" and that's when I cried out to God.

For Billy, pain and desperation drove him into the arms of God, and into a readiness to respond. Listen, God knows exactly what it takes to shake your world and move you into action.

So, whether you're experiencing feelings of aspiration or desperation, the idea is to listen for God's voice and to respond. That means you're going to have to take a step of faith.

Getting Practical: Closing "The Gap"

I'll never forget my first marathon back in 1996. In just six months, I went from being a couch potato, unable to run more than a couple of miles, to crossing the finish line of the Dallas Marathon.

The Last Chapter: Step of Faith

The big deal isn't that I stumbled through 26.2 miles to the finish line—thousands of people do that every year without the power of the Spirit. More significant was the discovery of three key Biblical principles for taking a step of faith (see below).

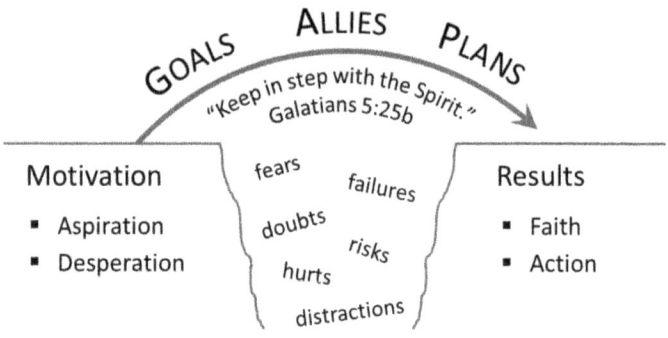

These three principles: Goals, Allies, and Plans (GAP), have changed how I approach taking any significant step of faith.

If you and I met for coffee and conversation, and you shared a specific step of faith from your LifeSigns, I'd ask you the three GAP questions:

- *What does your final destination look like?* (Goals)
- *Who's with you?* (Allies)
- *How will you get there?* (Plans)

Your answers to those three questions (or lack thereof), will reveal how likely you are to be successful. All three are critical, so let's spend a minute on each.

LifeSigns: How are you? Really.

#1 - Goals: Where are you going?

My freshman year in college, a roommate's parents put a sign over his desk. With an arrow flying randomly through space, it simply stated:

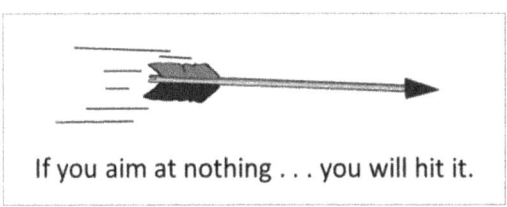

If you aim at nothing . . . you will hit it.

Even today, that sign makes me giggle. I suspect that my roommate's parents were trying to send a not-so-subtle message: "Don't just float through college. Find your passion, pick a major, and focus!"

Paul the apostle said essentially the same thing to an undisciplined bunch of believers in the Corinthian church: "Therefore I do not run like someone running aimlessly; I do not fight like a boxer beating the air" (1 Corinthians 9:26). Like my roommate's parents, Paul was telling his spiritual children down in Corinth, "Don't run aimlessly. Don't just swing wildly. Focus!"

If you look closely at the gospels, you'll find that Jesus had clear goals to guide his steps during His earthly ministry. He knew *why* He was here and *what* the Father wanted him to accomplish. And even though the disciples sometimes misunderstood His mission and motives, Jesus was crystal clear on His ultimate destination, and how He would get there.

Some of Jesus' goals encompassed the larger purpose of His life's work: "For the Son of Man came to seek and to save the lost" (Luke 19:10). The disciples were hoping the Messiah would free them from iron-fisted Roman rule.

Some of Jesus' goals provided guidelines for *how* He would operate in ministry: "For even the Son of Man did not come to be served, but to serve, and to give his life as a ransom for many"

The Last Chapter: Step of Faith

(Mark 10:45). You may remember the disciples were focused on who would be the greatest.

Sometimes Jesus used a contrast to more accurately describe his mission: "The thief comes only to steal and kill and destroy; I came that they may have life and have it abundantly" (John 10:10). People flocked to Jesus when He met their physical needs, but Jesus came to meet their spiritual needs as well.

Some of Jesus' goals were situation-specific and unpopular with the crowd. After healing dozens of people in Capernaum, Luke writes, "They tried to keep him from leaving them. But He said to them, 'I must preach the kingdom of God to the other cities also, for I was sent for this purpose'" (Luke 4:42).

Lastly, and perhaps most importantly, Jesus clearly understood *who* was calling the shots, even in the most difficult circumstances. The night before being tortured and humiliated on the cross, He said, "Now My soul has become troubled; and what shall I say, 'Father, save Me from this hour?' *But for this purpose I came to this hour*" (John 12:27). Then later He said, "Abba! Father! All things are possible for You; remove this cup from Me; yet not what I will, but what You will" (Mark 14:36).

Don't miss that last example. Jesus surrendered His will in exchange for the Father's will, even when it meant death on a cross. For Jesus, the essence of walking by faith meant submitting to His Father's goals, plans, and methods to redeem a lost world.

Where is God leading you?

Look again at each area in your LifeSigns: Relationships. Marriage. Money. Career. Kids. Finances.

If you haven't already done so, grab some paper and ask the Lord this question: *"God, I'm willing to follow wherever you lead me. What's the next step in this area of my life?"* Writing down your next steps can help solidify your goals and turn all those squishy wishes into firm commitments.

I don't know about you, but when I'm trying to discern God's will, I tend to over-think and over-complicate things. I tend to "lean on my own understanding" rather than trusting in God. Listen to how Jesus provides such simple, clear instructions to his disciples:

"Come to Me."[11]
"Listen to Me."
"Follow Me."
"Abide in Me."

Notice that each of these commands has two critical components: His invitation and our response. I often return to that familiar verse in Proverbs when asking God for direction: "Trust in the Lord with all your heart, and do not lean on your own understanding. In all your ways acknowledge Him and He will make your paths straight" (Proverbs 2:3-4). It's the perfect prescription for a step of faith.

I know there's much more to explore when it comes to understanding the Spirit's leadership in your life. If you'd like to learn more, pick up a copy of the excellent book *The Power of a Whisper*. It's packed with practical, Biblical wisdom.

#2 - ALLIES: WHO'S WITH YOU?

Our merry band of first-time marathoners met every Saturday morning for our long runs, pushing ourselves farther into the unknown week after week. Honestly, there's just no way I'd have tackled all those long runs by myself. We shared our stories, our struggles, and our little victories. We laughed till Gatorade came out our noses and we clung to each other for courage in the final miles. It was an unforgettable lesson in the power of Allies.

Wedged into that familiar scripture from Ecclesiastes, the one you hear at weddings about how, "Two are better than one," there lies a stern warning: "Woe to the one who falls when there is not another to lift him up" (Ecclesiastes 4:10b). Proverbs goes even

---

[11] For context, see Matthew 11:28, Mark 7:14, John 1:43, John 15:4

further to warn us about the perils of isolation, "He who separates himself seeks his own desire, he quarrels against all sound wisdom" (Proverbs 18:1). If nothing else comes from your LifeSigns experience, I'm hoping that you'll connect with someone who can "lift you up" when you fall.

Jesus had powerful Allies during his earthly trek. First and foremost, He had the Father and the Spirit. Skim the book of John and you'll find Jesus saying things like, "I do not speak on My own initiative, but the Father Himself who sent Me has given Me a commandment as to what to say and what to speak" (John 14:29). You'll also see the Spirit ministering to Him in the desert, and later in the garden of Gethsemane.

My kids love the Charlie Brown cartoon where Linus asks, *"Did Jesus have a dog?"* While I have no idea if Jesus had canine companionship (my kids are sure that He did), I do know that Jesus invested years in developing human companions.

Think about it. The twelve disciples were a group of hand-picked, intentionally developed, and carefully nurtured Allies. Peter, James, and John formed His inner circle. Look closely at the gospel of Luke and you might even catch a glimpse of Jesus' ministry support team: Mary Magdalene, Joanna, and Susanna. These faithful women "were helping to support them out of their own means…as Jesus traveled about from one town and village to another, proclaiming the good news of the kingdom of God" (Luke 8:1, 3).

You have powerful Allies too: the Father, the Son, the Spirit. Notice how all three are woven together into a powerful alliance of support:

> *"I will ask the Father, and He will give you another Helper, that He may be with you forever; that is the Spirit of truth, you know Him because He abides with you and will be in you"* (John 14:16-17).

That's right, Jesus called the Holy Spirit by the name of "Helper." Isn't that cool? The Bible includes more than 100 different names for God. All those names can help you understand His many attributes, character, and nature. Next time you're struggling to take a step of faith, try approaching God in a fresh way. Engage Him as your Helper. Counselor. Comforter. Advocate. Shepherd. Deliverer. Friend. Mediator. Refuge. Rock. Daddy (Abba). Teacher. Tower. Strength. (Google "names of God" for a complete list.)

What's more, even if you're not the outgoing type, you can develop powerful friendships. But just as the twelve disciples didn't corner Jesus in the temple and ask to be his friend, so too you need to prayerfully consider potential Allies, then take the initiative.

It's okay to pick Allies with an eye towards your God-given goals. When I needed help to start my first company, I reached out to David Dobat, Kurt Baxter, and my parents, Dick and Cindy Watson, to help craft a business plan. All of them had traveled the perilous road of entrepreneurship, dodging the potholes, and learning valuable lessons along the way.

Think about one of your goals identified in LifeSigns. Who can you enlist as an Ally? Who can you ask for help?

#3: PLANS – HOW WILL YOU GET THERE?

Running a marathon is less about race-day inspiration than it is about systematic preparation. When our little group started training, my longest run was four miles. So, I couldn't imagine running 26.2 miles at one time. When I thought about race day for very long, panic set in. But we had a proven plan. Over the span of 16 weeks, we would gradually increase the length of our long runs by just a mile or two, or by 10% each week. Soon, 10, 15, and 20-mile training runs were no big deal. What was utterly impossible a few months before, became possible when we followed the training plan. As race day loomed closer on the calendar, I took comfort in knowing we'd followed a well-researched, proven plan.

God is one heck of a strategic planner. The concept of strategic planning may be popular in the business world, but even the most brilliant people in multi-billion-dollar corporations have nothing on the strategic plan created by God. According to one expert, Jesus fulfilled more than 315 Old Testament prophecies as the Messiah, including His birth, life, death, and resurrection. Don't let the word "prophecy" throw you, it simply refers to those bits and pieces of God's strategic plan that He revealed to Biblical authors across the centuries. Those prophecies were sneak peeks at His elaborately crafted script of redemption, written by the hand of the Master.

Did you know that Jesus had a plan for his earthly ministry? Over and over, He told the disciples, "I'm here to do the Father's will." The Father's agenda was His agenda. The Father's priorities were His priorities. And the Father's plan was His plan.

Jesus said, "I do nothing on My own initiative, but I speak these things as *the Father taught Me*" (John 8:28). Jesus also said, "so the world may know that I love the Father, *I do exactly as the Father commanded Me*" (John 14:31).

And we learn in Matthew that, "Jesus began to explain to his disciples that he must go to Jerusalem and suffer many things at the hands of the elders, chief priests and teachers of the law, and that he must be killed and on the third day be raised to life" (Matthew 16:21).

Bottom Line: Jesus had a detailed and terrifying plan. Sometimes, I find it hard to believe that He followed through with it, knowing the horrors that awaited Him at the cross. Oh, how He must love us! Which leads us back to you. God tells us that He has plans for your life, "to give you hope and a future" (Jeremiah 29:11).

What's more, we know from the creation account that we share in God's nature and personality. God is a planner, and as those created in His image, we are planners too. Your methods and means of planning may differ from mine, but the act of looking into the future, prayerfully asking God to guide your steps, and using your God-given intellect to chart a course...it's all from Him. There's nothing unspiritual about it!

Rather than suggesting a template or method for planning, let's look to scripture for some guiding principles. Here are a few of the more helpful and practical verses on planning:

- *"The plans of the diligent lead surely to advantage"* (Proverbs 21:5). Notice, you gain an advantage when you're diligent in planning.

- *"The mind of man plans his way, But the Lord directs his steps"* (Proverbs 16:9). Notice the blend of your human plans and God's sovereign direction. Both are at work.

- Jesus spoke of the wisdom of planning with this parable: *"For which one of you, when he wants to build a tower, does not first sit down and calculate the cost to see if he has enough to complete it? Otherwise, when he has laid a foundation and is not able to finish, all who observe it begin to ridicule him, saying, 'This man began to build and was not able to finish.' Or what king, when he sets out to meet another king in battle, will not first sit down and consider whether he is strong enough with ten thousand men to encounter the one coming against him with twenty thousand?"* (Luke 14:28-32).

NEXT STEPS: HOW CAN YOU OBEY TODAY?

Goals. Allies. Plans. Three powerful, biblical principles that can help you turn aspirations into actions. They will serve you well in following Jesus, wherever He's leading you. Now, do you want to hear the rest of Billy's story? It's wonderful.

The Last Chapter: Step of Faith

When I cried out to God, Mercy Ships came into my mind as clear as can be. When Mercy Ships came into my mind I questioned why. In my heart God spoke to me and said, "I am about to put you on a path that will reveal a side of you that you have never known before." That was enough for me. I called Julie as she was getting ready to leave for Africa. That I caught her at home was practically an act of God in itself. We talked about 5 minutes, she gave me some basic info and I went home and wrote out my resignation. I didn't really know what Mercy Ships was, I didn't know where it was, and I didn't know what the Crossroads school was. I just knew I was supposed to go. That wasn't as much of a step of faith as I knew if things didn't change, I was a dead man. So, I resigned in March not knowing I wouldn't leave until September. But I went because I knew that I knew that I knew what God had said.

Did you catch that? Billy says, *"I knew…that I knew…that I knew what God had said."* And Billy followed through, completing a demanding six-month missions training program. He later become the executive chef at Mercy Ships' global training center. Over the last dozen years, Billy has continued to take steps of faith. I've seen God transform his heart, use his gifts to touch thousands of people, develop his skills as a master chef and writer, and integrate him into the fabric of our family. It all started with a five-minute phone call, prompted by God's grace, enabled by God's power, and wrapped in God's plan for Billy's life.

You may be struggling with the "Next Steps" recorded in your LifeSigns Growth Plan. Most folks do. I hear things like, "I just don't know God's will for my life," or, "I'm praying for clarity before I do anything." Fair enough, those are good prayers. But whether your next steps are clear or not, may I make a simple suggestion?

Do whatever is next. Obey today.

LifeSigns: How are you? Really.

In my experience, a Spirit-led step of faith usually only requires a "baby step," rather than a flying leap into the abyss of the unknown. *Baby steps can be big steps.*

Over the years, I've taken a baby step by walking over to the sink and pouring out a full bottle of alcohol. By faith, more times than I'll readily admit, I've picked up the phone and told someone, "I was wrong. I'm sorry. Can we talk?" By faith, as I struggled to develop the very first version of LifeSigns, I asked some very busy men and women to give me their time, feedback, and wise counsel. And by faith, I still choose to get into my car and drive to recovery meetings, choosing to be candid and honest with a circle of men who are doing the same.

Little steps lead to big victories.

For me, this whole "step of faith" business follows a predictable cycle: the tension builds, I resist, I suffer the consequences of inaction, and finally, I move. There's usually an immediate sense of joy, blessing, and relief. That's why at the end of James' explanation of faith and action, he writes, "Whoever looks intently into the perfect law that gives freedom, and continues in it—not forgetting what they have heard, but doing it—*they will be blessed in what they do.*" Notice that James says the blessing comes after the "doing."

Here's a sure sign of spiritual growth in your life: Are you resisting less—and responding more to the Spirit's nudge? That's it. That's the whole ball game, my friend.

Nudge, respond. Nudge, respond.

Don't worry if the Lord hasn't revealed the entire plan for your future, only the first step. I think God does that on purpose. He wants you to learn to how trust Him, and He wants to make the journey with you. So just take that next step in faith.

Nudge, respond. Nudge, respond.

The Last Chapter: Step of Faith

And, have goals, allies, and plans. Doing so will increase your odds of success exponentially. When we get to our heavenly home, I'm going to ask the Lord to pull back the curtain and reveal how, "The steps of a man are established by the Lord. When he falls, he will not be hurled headlong, because the Lord is the One who holds his hand." (Psalm 37:23-24).

I can almost see Him holding my hand.

In the meantime, my shaky steps will be by faith.

Frequently Asked Questions

"Must I participate in LifeSigns?"

No, you do not have to participate. LifeSigns is totally voluntary and is not required for participation in church programs, for service or leadership roles, or for general church membership.

"Is this confidential? Who will see it?"

Your individual LifeSigns is totally confidential. Nobody at your church will see your individual responses unless you share your results with them. This is a candid conversation between you and God. Your church has contracted with an independent firm to collect responses, create profiles, and provide LifeSigns profiles in a secure, 100% confidential manner.

As an added precaution, none of your data is be stored on church computers or servers. It cannot be accessed by leaders or staff at your church. Only numerical averages and aggregate data will be rolled into a summary for use by leaders to better understand and meet the needs of the body. No written responses or comments will be used in summary reports.

Appendix A: Frequently Asked Questions

"How does the LifeSigns process work?"

Step 1: Take your LifeSigns and get your 20-page Growth Plan. You'll need anywhere from 20 to 40 minutes of quiet, uninterrupted time for your "Vertical conversation." We do not recommend taking your LifeSigns while you're at work.

Step 2: Read chapters 1-3 of this book on the why, what, and how of LifeSigns. You'll get a solid biblical foundation on how to have the "Two Conversations" and discover how it can change your life.

Step 3: Have a "Horizontal Conversation" with someone you trust, share your top growth priorities, and identify specific next steps. Pray for each other and agree to check-in over the next several weeks to share updates and encouragement.

"How honest should I be?"

Please be totally honest with yourself and with God. Many of us look good on the outside but are hurting or broken on the inside. LifeSigns is an opportunity to step back and reflect on your life in light of biblical truth.

Keep in mind that any truly candid conversation may involve some degree of discomfort. You may feel uncertain how to respond. On our best days, we all demonstrate many of the qualities we ask about in LifeSigns…but on our worst days, we demonstrate very few of them. Try to think about your life on *most* days. Focus on how it's going right now.

Remember, this is not a test, it's a conversation with God. "The Lord doesn't see things the way you see them. People judge by outward appearance, but the Lord looks at the heart" (1 Samuel 16:7). Pray for guidance and be as candid as possible in both your vertical and horizontal conversations. As thousands of people have discovered, it's totally worth it.

"What's the real agenda here?"

To help each of us take the next steps in our spiritual walk. That's it. This is not church marketing research; it's not a theology test. LifeSigns is simply a spiritual growth tool for you and your church family. What's more, because no one else will see your individual responses, you're free to drop your guard and simply be yourself.

As with most things, you will get out of LifeSigns what you put into it. So put your whole heart into it.

"What's in my LifeSigns Growth Plan?"

Once you've completed your LifeSigns "vertical conversation" on-line, the system will e-mail you a confidential 20-page Growth Plan that includes:
- a summary of your LifeSigns for each area
- all your written comments
- a list of your self-selected priorities for growth
- specially selected scripture and growth resources matched to your personal priorities
- a LifeSigns conversation guide you can use with a friend, if you so choose
- your next steps for each area

"I'm a small group leader. Give me some ideas for the Horizontal Conversation."

You don't have to cover all the topics in this book. Keep in mind that the twelve chapters labeled "conversation starters" address all the major topics in LifeSigns, but some may not apply to your group (e.g., being out of work, having kids, etc.). Feel free to have your group pick and choose the topics they're most interested in covering.

Some small groups will choose to work through all the topics over a period of 8-10 weeks. It's up to you.

Other groups are using just one section, such as the Marriage section, as preparation for a retreat or marriage conference. Please be sure to share your creative ideas for how your small group is having candid conversations with your pastor.

APPENDIX A: FREQUENTLY ASKED QUESTIONS

"I ATTEND ANOTHER CHURCH. HOW CAN WE USE LIFESIGNS?"

LifeSigns can be customized to meet the unique needs of any church. It's also available to small groups and individuals as a discipleship tool.

If you, or your church, would like to explore how to deploy LifeSigns, please contact:

Scott Watson
LifeSigns Partners, Inc.
214-535-5774
scott@myLifeSigns.org

Please visit myLifeSigns.org to learn more.

LifeSigns Methodology

"How was LifeSigns developed?"

Chapters 1 and 2 include an overview of how LifeSigns was developed. For those interested, here's a little more of the backstory and methodology.

In the fall of 2008, a spiritual assessment team at Bent Tree Bible Fellowship in Carrollton, Texas, led by pastor Michelle Attar, reviewed surveys conducted by leading churches from around the country. After careful review, analysis, and much prayer, it was determined that none of the existing surveys would accomplish the primary objective: To enable every person to deeply explore their life with Christ, share those insights with another person, and identify specific next steps.

In February of 2009, a total of 141 Bent Tree staff and volunteers completed a LeaderView® profile to help identify "the hallmarks of a maturing disciple." The results provided the basis for creating the first generation of the LifeSigns® tool and process. A project team that included pastors, leaders, and members of the

Appendix B: LifeSigns Methodology

church provided written and verbal feedback on the early versions of LifeSigns content and flow.

Three pilots of LifeSigns were conducted with members, leaders, staff, and non-church members. The current version (v13.1) of LifeSigns went through seven major revisions and dozens of minor revisions to the content, flow, layout, and language. LifeSigns truly is a product of believers working together as a body.

You'll find that the LifeSigns questions are almost always worded as positive attributes, rather than negative statements. This is intentional. For example, we use a positive question like, "Do your relationships feel safe, where you can be authentic and talk about real life?" rather than its negative equivalent of, "Are your relationships shallow?" This keeps our focus on the signs of life, instead of the consequences of sin. Negative descriptions are only used to create a sense of contrast in some of the examples provided after the questions (e.g., "...you feel safe sharing your struggles – rather than putting on a happy face and pretending that everything is fine.").

LifeSigns questions are often a hybrid of both affective (emotional) indicators and behavioral indicators. For example, we ask "How often do your relationships *feel* safe?" This enables participants to more accurately reflect on their actual experience, without feeling condemned or judged by the survey process. This hybrid technique also addresses the preferences of a broader range of personality types (thinkers and feelers).

Finally, we resisted the temptation to preach via the survey, and we've avoided the use of theological terminology wherever possible. Our goal was to translate the purity of scriptural truths into everyday language, accessible to a large number of people.

Questions about Spirit-lead worship, evangelism, or sanctification are placed into a familiar context of everyday life situations, such as handling money, work, and marriage.

Behind every LifeSigns question there are specific scriptures, and in some cases, whole chapters of the Bible. Once the LifeSigns survey data has been collected, the individual LifeSigns Growth Plans place each question back into its appropriate spiritual category, complete with the related scripture reference. This book also contains many, but not all, of the scriptures behind each LifeSigns question.

To learn more, please visit myLifeSigns.org.